MUHAMMAD

The Last Messenger

CHILDREN'S SERIES

SENIOR LEVEL - PART II

ʿĀLIA N. AṬHAR

LIBRARY OF ISLAM
P. O. Box 1923
Des Plaines, Illinois 60017 (U.S. A.)

First published by Library of Islam
P.O. Box 1923
Des Plaines, Illinois 60017-1923 (U.S.A.)

DISTRIBUTOR:
Kazi Publications Inc.
3023 West Belmont Avenue
Chicago, Illinois 60618 (U.S.A.)

AUTHOR:
Aṭhar, ʿĀlia N.

MUḤAMMAD, The Last Messenger II
(Ṣalla Allāhu ʻalaihi wa Ṣallam)

ISBN: 0-934905-06-1

TYPESETTING:
A-1 Typesetters, Chicago

Manufactured in the United States of America

1 2 3 4 5 6 7 8 9 10

CONTENTS

Author's Note			4
Foreword			5
Lesson	1	The Blessed Travelers	9
Lesson	2	Foundation of the First Mosque	13
Lesson	3	The Great Welcome	16
Lesson	4	Beginning of the Islamic Era	20
Lesson	5	The Peace Agreement of Madīnah	26
Lesson	6	The Hypocrites (*Munāfiqūn*)	30
Lesson	7	The Order for Self-Defense: *Jihād*	34
Lesson	8	Establishment of the Muslim Community	39
Lesson	9	The Miracle at Badr	44
Lesson	10	The Challenges	51
Lesson	11	The Uhud Encounter	56
Lesson	12	Obedience to Allāh is Essential for Success	63
Lesson	13	Plot Against the Prophet (s.a.w.)	68
Lesson	14	The Allied Opposition	72
Lesson	15	Treaty of Ḥudaybiyah	79
Lesson	16	Invitation to Other Kingdoms	84
Lesson	17	Return to Makkah	90
Lesson	18	Islamization of Makkah	94
Lesson	19	The Last Expeditions	100
Lesson	20	The Farewell Pilgrimage (*Ḥajjat-ul-Wadā'*)	106
Lesson	21	Completion of the Mission	110

بسم الله الرحمن الرحيم

AUTHOR'S NOTE

The present work is a response to the demand for an appropriate text b on *Sirah,* the life-history of Prophet Muhammad (s.a.w.). It is meant to se not only the immediate need of Muslim educational centers but also to fill void at American public schools on this vital subject.

In view of the particular audience for these books, the use of Ara terminology has been restricted, except where it was necessary to emphas certain concepts. The senior level books in this series are recommended readers between the age of ten and fifteen years. Volumes I and II on the *Sir* provide an account of Makkah and Madinah periods, respectively.

Wa ma tawfiqi illa billah (and my success in my task can come fro Allah only).

Chicago 'Alia N. Athar

بسم الله الرحمن الرحيم

FOREWORD

IN THE NAME OF ALLĀH, THE BENEFICENT, THE MERCIFUL

It is heartening to note that in recent years, there has been a marked expansion of the Muslim community in the West. The universal nature of Islām and its emphasis on the practical aspects which encompasses the total life of the individual has been the driving force during this whole process. It would not be an overestimate to say that the Muslims in the West are taking a leading role in transforming the world into a peaceful abode for everybody. No doubt, the present crisis in the world is the result of distancing ourselves too much from the spiritual aspects of our existence.

To reach the lofty goal of existing in a peaceful world, it is important that the essence of the religion of Islām be internalized in its truest sense. This requires the wide urgency of availability of Islamic literature in this environment. Although attention has been directed towards this end and some work has been done, there is a visible dearth of appropriate literature for children and youth. They are growing up in an atmosphere which is distinctly different from the one in which their parents grew up. They have specific needs, which require specific attention.

It is now time for this issue to be addressed properly, before our young generation is totally alienated from their religious background. In a society, where an adolescent is exposed to a variety of experiences, an awareness of his/her religious and cultural heritage is but a deterrent to his/her being lost in the conflicting milieu. It is incumbent upon us to help the Muslim children and youth to understand and relate to themselves and others so as to exist as healthy and productive human-beings, making optimal contribution to the well-being of the society.

With a demanding new generation of Muslims, reaching the stage of adolescence, the task of educating them becomes a major responsibility of the parents. Also, it puts an enormous strain on the intellectual sources of the community. The challenge lies with the Muslim educationists who must measure up to the task of introducing the basics of Islām to children growing up in a changing, challenging and complex world. They have to make the material so appealing that it draws immediate attention of the inquisitive child of this age and enhances and motivates learning.

This work is a part of the series of books that Dr. ʿĀlia N. Aṭhar aspires to present to the young readers. I am confident that her knowledge and expertise in the field and her commitment and devotion to the task would enable her to carry on her plan successfully. Her endeavours to contribute to the training of young minds are highly appreciable. I believe that the books in this series would be of great value.

I pray to Almighty Allāh to help the author in bringing this series to completion and make it beneficial for the community.

Dr. ʿAbdullāh ʿOmar Naṣeef
Secretary General
Rābiṭat al-ʿĀlam al-Islāmī
Makkah al-Mukarramah
Kingdom of Saʿūdi Arabia

Rajab 27, 1407
March 28, 1987

TO

MUJAHIDIN

All over the world.

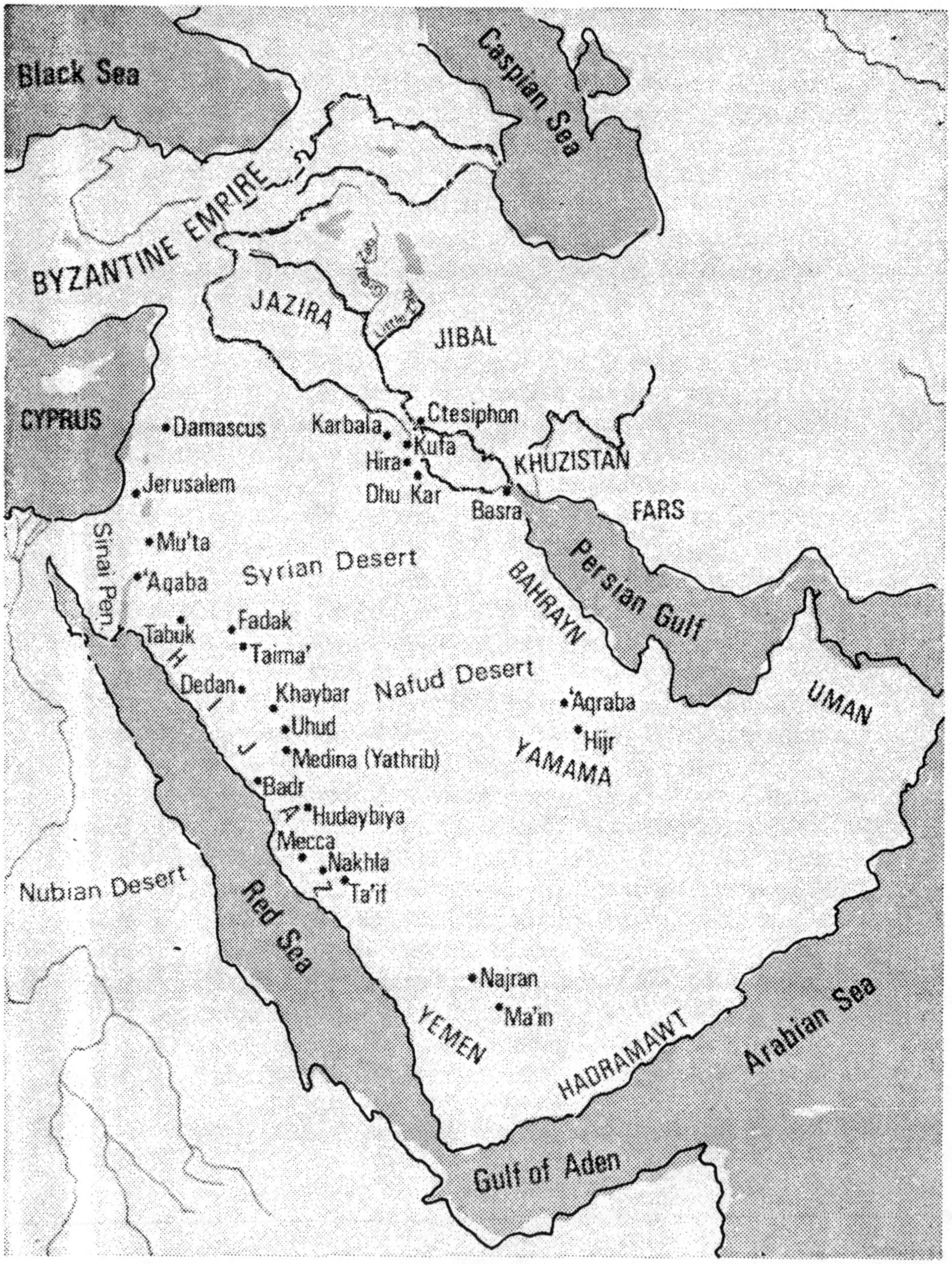

Map of Arabia showing important cities.

LESSON 1

THE BLESSED TRAVELERS

In the midst of bitter opposition and severe hardships, Prophet Muḥammad (s.a.w.) preached Islam in Makkah for thirteen years. At last, the order came from Allāh to migrate for the sake of Islām. By this time, a significant number of people in Yathrib (a town, about six hundred kilometers to the north-east of Makkah) had embraced Islām. The Prophet (s.a.w.) asked the Muslims to migrate to Yathrib and himself preferred to stay in Makkah until all of the Muslims had gone to Yathrib.

Enraged and puzzled over the migration of the Muslims, the Makkan leaders decided to assassinate the Prophet of Islām (s.a.w.) and assigned this task to a group of young men representing many tribes and clans. They besieged the Prophet's house and vowed to kill him when he came out at dawn. Almighty Allāh informed His Prophet (s.a.w.) about the evil plan of the Makkans and enabled him to leave the house miraculously, without being seen by the enemies who were guarding his house with extreme caution.

While Alī ibn Abū Ṭālib slept in the Prophet's bed and took the responsibility of returning the valuables which the Makkans had kept in the custody of the Prophet (s.a.w.), the Prophet went to the house of his devoted *Ṣaḥābī* (Companion), Abū Bakr, and both of them left Makkah. In order to defend themselves against the enemies who were desperately searching for them everywhere, they hid in the cave of Thawr for three days. Then they resumed their tiresome journey to Yathrib.

The Muslims in Yathrib had received the news that Prophet Muhammad (s.a.w.) was on his way and they were waiting for his arrival anxiously. There were the *Anṣār* (the local people of Yathrib), who had already met with the Prophet (s.a.w.), and were so influenced by his nobility and truth, that they had accepted the religion of Islām wholeheartedly. With dedication and sincerity, they had made Islām popular in Yathrib. They had recognized the majesty of Islām and the fact that Muḥammad (s.a.w.) was the true Prophet who could save them and their community from destruction.

In greater numbers were the *Anṣār* who until now had not met with the Last Messenger of Allāh (s.a.w.), whose name was included in their daily prayers and who cared for nothing but the mission assigned to him from Almighty Allāh. They had accepted his message to be guided towards the path of glory in this world as well as the *Ākhirah* (the Hereafter). They had the honor of inviting the Messenger (s.a.w.) and his followers to their city so as to participate in the glorious task of establishing the true religion on earth.

Among the people waiting for the Prophet (s.a.w.) were the *Muhājirūn* (the Makkan Muslims), who had been persecuted and harassed by the people of their own city and had migrated to Yathrib to enjoy the freedom of practicing Islām. Muḥammad (s.a.w.) had been brought up among them. He was the most perfect example of a human being, whom Almighty Allāh had chosen to direct the people from the darkness of evil to the light of goodness. He was the one who had brought a complete change in their lives, from continual tribal fights and cruelty, to harmony, kindness and love.

In a brief period of a few years, he had been successful to get them out of the habits of the period of *Jāhiliyyah* (ignorance) and follow the refined system of Islam. How quickly they had forgotten their tribal and racial differences and had united under the leadership of the Messenger of Allāh (s.a.w.)! The only goal ahead of them was the pleasure of Allāh and His obedience. They had abandoned all false worshippings and false standards of pride of the days of *Jāhiliyyah*.

They had endured the worst tortures with iron will and strong faith in the religion of Islām. The stories of their patience and steadfastness were on the lips of the people of Arabia. Not only that, but they had also sacrificed their homeland and their relatives for the sake of the true religion. By leaving their possessions in Makkah willingly, they had proved that the pleasure and obedience of Allāh was the most important objective for them. In a materialistic society, there could not be a greater example of faith and trust in the Creator.

There were the non-believers, who had not accepted Islām but were curious to see the man who was adored by the Muslims more than their own parents. Moreover, they shared with the Muslims the feelings to have a leader who could resolve their internal differences and give them a peaceful atmosphere, where no one would be worried about the security of his life or property.

Every morning, the *Anṣār* and the *Muhājirūn* would come out of the city and assemble at Thāniyat-al-Wadā', a hill in the south of the town of Qubā'. Qubā' was about five kilometers from Yathrib and was inhabited by a clan of the'Awf tribe, Banū 'Amr ibn 'Awf. All of them used to wait eagerly for the Prophet Muḥammad (s.a.w.) sharing their delight over the Blessings from Almighty Allāh. After many hours, when the sun rays would become unbearable, they would return to their homes disappointed.

Finally, the happiest moment came. A small caravan in the desert route was moving towards the town. The Muslims' joy knew no bounds. They called their friends and everyone got ready to welcome the Messenger of Allāh. With great enthusiasm and elation, they received the Prophet (s.a.w.) and his *Ṣaḥābah* (Companions). Their shouts of *Allāhu Akbar* (Allāh is Great) informed everyone in the city that the one who had been awaited so anxiously had arrived. They thanked Allāh for His Mercy upon them. Also, at this moment of elation, they changed the name of Yathrib to *Madīnat-un-Nabī* (the City of the Prophet).

This was a time of special celebration for the Muslims. No longer was there worry about the safety of their beloved Prophet (s.a.w.) who was left in Makkah surrounded by his worst enemies. The time for the fulfilment of the promise of Allāh had drawn nearer. During *Mi'rāj,* the Prophet (s.a.w.) had been honored with the *Waḥī* (Revelation):

وَقُلْ جَآءَ ٱلْحَقُّ وَزَهَقَ ٱلْبَٰطِلُ ۚ إِنَّ ٱلْبَٰطِلَ كَانَ زَهُوقًا ﴿٨١﴾

And say: the truth has come, the falsehood perished;
Falsehood was bound to perish.

al-Isrā'
17: 81

Every scheme of the Quraysh to stop the tide of Islām had been futile. The Prophet (s.a.w.) was safe and sound and was looking forward to the time when there would not remain a single idol-worshipper. He had passed through his trials with unparalleled perseverance and unshaken faith in Almighty Allāh. His successful migration to Madīnah was a supreme example of the victory of truth over falsehood.

EXERCISE 1

A. Read each of the following statements carefully and circle the correct answer: a, b, c, or d.

1. Prophet Muhammad (s.a.w.) traveled to Yathrib-----
   a. in the company of Abū Bakr.
   b. in the company of ʿAlī ibn Abū Ṭālib.
   c. in the company of many Muslims.
   d. all alone.

2. At the time of Muslim migration to Yathrib----
   a. all of the people of Yathrib had accepted Islām.
   b. nobody in Yathrib had accepted Islām.
   c. many people in Yathrib had accepted Islām.

3. The *Muhājirūn* were the Muslims who-----
   a. were the local people of Yathrib.
   b. had endured tortures for the sake of Islām.
   c. had migrated from Makkah to Yathrib.
   d. b and c.

B. Answer the following questions.

1. Why did the *Anṣār* invite Prophet Muḥammad (s.a.w.) to their city?
2. What is the meaning of the term, 'Days of Ignorance'?
3. How did the Muslims welcome the Prophet?

LESSON 2

FOUNDATION OF THE FIRST MOSQUE

Prophet Muḥammad (s.a.w.) stayed in Qubā' for one or two weeks. His devout friend and devoted follower, Abū Bakr Siddīq, who had accompanied him through the most dangerous and tedious journey, remained with him throughout this period. Prophet's cousin, 'Alī ibn Abū Ṭālib, who had left Makkah after returning the assets of the people to their rightful owners, joined him here.

He brought the news that the families of the Prophet (s.a.w.) and Abū Bakr would soon be on their way to Madīnah. Zayd ibn Ḥāritha was leading the party which consisted of his wife, Zaynab, the Prophet's wife, Sawdah, and his daughters, Fāṭimah and Umm Kulthūm. 'Abdullāh ibn Abū Bakr's party included his mother, Umm Rumān, and his two sisters, 'Āisha and 'Asmā.

People began coming in groups to give an enthusiastic welcome to the Prophet (s.a.w.) and his *Ṣaḥābah.* The Prophet (s.a.w.) spent each and every moment of his time in teaching the people the principles of Islām, especially morality and good behavior. He also attended to the problems of the local community which the people brought to him. They were extremely happy to have the Prophet (s.a.w.) among them and listened to every word uttered by him carefully.

During this brief period, the Prophet (s.a.w.) laid the foundation of a mosque. All of the *Ṣaḥābah* participated in this sacred task. Apparently, it was a small hut, but one can imagine the greatness of the mosque which was the first mosque founded in Islām by the Messenger of Allāh (s.a.w.). This mosque is called *Masjid-ul-Qubā'* and is very much revered by the Muslims who do not forget to pray there whenever they pay a visit to the City of the Prophet (s.a.w.).

It was Friday morning when the Prophet (s.a.w.) and his *Ṣaḥābah* resumed their journey to Madīnah. By noon, they reached the locality where the clan of Banū Salīm ibn 'Awf lived. The Prophet (s.a.w.) decided to go down there and perform congregational prayer in the mosque which the local Muslims had already built there. It was the first prayer that the Prophet (s.a.w.) led with a *Khuṭbah* (sermon). This mosque is known as *Masjid-ul-Jum'a* and can be visited in the suburb of Madīnah.

The *Khuṭbah,* that the Prophet (s.a.w.) delivered on that historical day, was the first Friday *Khuṭbah* in the history of Islām. Almost one hundred people participated in this congregation. The *Khuṭbah* was of historical significance and was preserved carefully by the Muslims. Some of the important points of the *Khuṭbah* are the following:

1. The best advice a Muslim can give to another Muslim is to fear Allāh and be pious. There is nothing better than it. This is the source of strength in this world and in the Hereafter.
2. Avoid what Allāh has ordered you to avoid.
3. Your relationship to Allāh should be based on sincerity, nobility and truth. Such a relationship is possible only when your objective is to seek the pleasure of Allāh, and nothing else. This will enable you to get honor in this world as well as in the Hereafter.
4. Allāh is Compassionate, Truthful, and Merciful, and He fulfills His Promise, as He has told us in al-Qur'ān.
5. Allāh forgives the person who fears Him. Such a person is given many rewards from Allāh.
6. The person who obeys Allāh and has a sincere relationship with Him, will be protected against evil.
7. Allāh has all powers and He alone is the Master and the Lord of the Worlds. You should keep a relationship with Allāh in the right way and should not worry about others, as Allāh is the Greatest Protector of all.

The Prophet delivered this *Khuṭbah* when he and his followers were in the process of migrating from their home city to Madīnah. They had suffered too much at the hands of the *Kuffār*. For no less than thirteen years, the Prophet (s.a.w.) endured all kinds of physical and mental tortures only for the right to preach people to obey Allāh. He was beaten up, stones and dirt were thrown at him, insulting remarks hurled at him, and murderous attempts were made on his life.

Now, he was out of the territory of the *Kuffār* and was among his dedicated followers. Yet, the *Khuṭbah* had not the slightest reference to his or his followers' sufferings or any kind of revenge from his enemies who had driven him and his followers out of the city of their fore-fathers. The Blessing for humankind could not utter any words against anyone. His *Khutbah* focused only upon the essential teachings of Islām with the same sincerity, piety, and selflessness with which he had started his mission.

EXERCISE 2

A. Read each of the following statements carefully and circle T if the statement is true or F if it is false.

1. The Prophet (s.a.w.) left Makkah with his family. T/F
2. The Prophet (s.a.w.) stayed in Qubā' for many months. T/F
3. The first mosque established by the Prophet (s.a.w.) was in Qubā'. T/F
4. 'Alī ibn Abū Ṭālib joined the Prophet (s.a.w.) in Qubā'. T/F
5. The Prophet (s.a.w.) himself built *Masjid-ul-Jum'a.* T/F
6. In his *Khuṭbah* the Prophet (s.a.w.) complained about the *Kuffār*. T/F
7. The first *Khuṭbah* was attended by only ten Muslims. T/F
8. In order to please Almighty Allāh, we must be pious and sincere. T/F
9. Our best Protector is Allāh. T/F
10. Our greatest source of strength is our faith in the Almighty. T/F

B. Answer the following questions.

1. How did the Prophet (s.a.w.) spend his time in Qubā'?
2. What is the significance of *Masjid-ul-Jum'a* for the Muslims?
3. Write down a summary of the first Friday *Khuṭbah* of the Prophet.

LESSON 3

THE GREAT WELCOME

The Muslims in Madīnah were rejoicing the safe arrival of the Prophet (s.a.w.). Everyone came out in his best dress to celebrate this happy event. Small boys and girls held their drums and sang welcome songs in chorus:

> The full moon rises from Thāniyat-ul-Wadā‘
> To spread its light on all of us.
> We must always thank Allāh,
> Until the time we can pray.
> O you, sent Divinely to us,
> Your commandment shall be obeyed.

The notables of the city requested the Prophet (s.a.w.) to stay in their quarters and enjoy the comfort and hospitality there. Every family was eager to be the host of the Prophet (s.a.w.). Delegations after delegations came to invite him to their respective localities. Since the Prophet (s.a.w.) did not want to hurt anybody, he decided to let his she-camel go free and stay at the place where it stopped. As he rode the she-camel, the people gave way to it, excited to see the place it chose to stop. At every step, the Prophet (s.a.w.) was again and again requested by the people to be their guest, but he gave the same answer to everyone.

The she-camel started running, with groups of people on both of its sides. It wandered in the quarters of Banū Najjār for sometime, and then sat down in an open space. The choice had beeb made. The Prophet (s.a.w.) inquired about the owner of the land. Mu‘ādh ibn Adra told him that the piece of land belonged to two orphans named Sahl and Suhayl, who were related to him and were living with him.

Mu‘ādh assured the Prophet (s.a.w.) that he had no objection if the Prophet took possession of the land and said that he would convince his relative orphans. The Prophet (s.a.w.) answered that he would take possession of the land only if it could be bought from its owners. At once, Abū Bakr paid the price of the land and it was purchased. Later, on the same piece of land, the Prophet's Mosque, *Masjid-un-Nabawī,* was founded.

By this time, the new name of Yathrib, *Madīnat-un-Nabī,* had become popular in the whole city. It seemed that not only was the name of the city changed but it had also gone through a complete transformation, emerging as a different city. Forgetting their old rivalries, the people were happily trying to outdo one another in greeting their Prophet and demonstrating their hospitality.

The Prophet (s.a.w.) decided to stay with Abū Ayyūb Anṣārī, whose house was closest to the place where the she-camel had stopped. Abū Ayyūb and his wife rejoiced the unexpected honor. They moved to the upper floor of the house so as to let the people visit the Prophet (s.a.w.) without any disturbance. The Prophet (s.a.w.) stayed in this house until the time when the Mosque was completed. Then he moved to his *Ḥujrah* (the residential part of the Mosque).

The *Hijrah* (migration) of the Prophet (s.a.w.) from Makkah to Madīnah is a milestone in the history of Islām. On the night of *Isrā'* and *Mi'rāj* (the Divine Journey), Almighty Allāh had revealed the Prayer to the Prophet (s.a.w.):

وَقُل رَّبِّ أَدْخِلْنِي مُدْخَلَ صِدْقٍ وَأَخْرِجْنِي مُخْرَجَ صِدْقٍ وَاجْعَل لِّي
مِن لَّدُنكَ سُلْطَانًا نَّصِيرًا ﴿٨٠﴾

> And say: My Lord! let my entry be by the Gate of Truth and Honor, and likewise, my exit by the Gate of Truth and Honor; and grant me from Your Presence, an authority to support me.
>
> al-Isrā'
> 17: 80

Almighty Allāh had guided the Muslims that they should have their complete trust in Him and should pray to Him for His help and support. They should not be afraid of the worldly powers in practicing their religion as Allāh's Power is over and above them. Allāh has clearly stated that temporary comforts and benefits in this world will be of no use to us in the *Ākhirah* (the Hereafter). So, we should not be hesitant in sacrificing them for the Sake of Allāh.

The most important aspect of our lives is our freedom to practice our faith, and we must endeavor to retain it at any cost. We should not hesitate in abandoning our most precious possessions, if they are obstacles in performing our duties to Almighty Allāh. Migrating to another place is a sacrifice a Muslim should make if there is no other alternative left. Al-Qur'ān says:

وَٱلَّذِينَ هَاجَرُوا۟ فِى ٱللَّهِ مِنۢ بَعْدِ مَا ظُلِمُوا۟
لَنُبَوِّئَنَّهُمْ فِى ٱلدُّنْيَا حَسَنَةً وَلَأَجْرُ ٱلْءَاخِرَةِ أَكْبَرُ لَوْ كَانُوا۟ يَعْلَمُونَ ﴿٤١﴾

Those who made *Hijrah* for the sake of Allāh, after they were oppressed, We will surely give them good home in this world; and surely, the reward of the Hereafter is even greater than that, if they only realize this.

an-Nahl
16: 41

« إِنَّ اللَّـهَ يَقُولُ يَوْمَ القِيَامَةِ : أَيْنَ
المُتَحَابُّونَ بِجَلالِي ؟ اليَوْمَ أُظِلُّهُمْ فِي ظِلِّي يَوْمَ لا
ظِلَّ إِلاَّ ظِلِّي » .

Where are those who love one another through My glory? Today I shall give them shade in My shade, it being a day when there is no shade but My shade.

It was related by al-Bukhārī (also by Mālik).

EXERCISE 3

A. Read each of the following statements carefully and circle the correct answer: a, b, c, or d.

1. The Prophet (s.a.w.) did not accept anyone's offer to be his guest because -----
   a. he had his arrangements already made.
   b. he did not like to hurt anyone's feelings.
   c. he did not want to stay in Madīnah.
   d. he did not like to stay with anyone.

2. At the time of the Prophet's entry into Madīnah, Muslims ----------
   a. were greatly delighted.
   b. gave him a superb welcome.
   c. showed their excellent hospitality.
   d. All of the above.

B. Answer the following questions.
1. How did the children of Madīnah welcome the Messenger of Allāh?
2. Where did the Prophet (s.a.w.) decide to stay?
3. What is the importance of *Hijrah* in Islām?

« قَالَ اللهُ عَزَّ وَجَلَّ : الْكِبْرِياءُ رِدائـي ، وَالْعَظَمَـةُ
إزارِي ، فَمَنْ نَازَعَنِي واحِداً مِنهُما ، قَذَفْتُهُ فِي النَّارِ» .

Pride is My cloak and greatness
My robe, and he who competes with
Me in respect of either of them I shall
cast into Hell-fire.

It was related by Abū Dāwūd (also by Ibn Mājah and Aḥmad) with sound chains of authority.

LESSON 4

BEGINNING OF THE ISLAMIC ERA

1 A.H.

The Muslims have a tradition that whenever they choose a place as their new abode, they simultaneously care for a mosque in the neighboring area. This tradition springs from the fact that the first task of the Prophet (s.a.w.) was his attention towards the construction of a mosque, which was built on the piece of land bought from Sahl and Suhayl.

In building the Mosque, the Prophet (s.a.w.) worked with his hands as did the *Anṣār* and the *Muhājirūn.* While laboring hard during the construction, they sang:

There is no life but the life of the next world.
O Allāh, have Mercy upon the *Anṣār* and the *Muhājirūn.*

The *Ṣaḥābah* requested the Prophet (s.a.w.) to rest and let them do the labor, but the latter refused. As a matter of fact, he worked harder than the others. They brought date trunks to make pillars of the Mosque and built the walls with stones and mud bricks. The Prophet's active participation encouraged the Muslims to work hard to complete the construction of the Mosque within a very short period. One of the *Ṣaḥābah* rhymed:

If we sat down while the Prophet worked,
It could be said that we shirked work.

The Mosque was simple but elegant. The four walls of its vast courtyard were built out of bricks and mud. One of its parts was covered with a ceiling. Another part was covered to serve as a platform to provide shelter to the poor who had no homes and spent most of their time in worship and supplication. These people are known as *Aṣḥāb-uṣ-Ṣuffah.* The Prophet (s.a.w.) expressed great affection for these people and attended to their needs especially.

This place in *Masjid-un-Nabawī* became the shelter for all those religious people who were homeless, and also those who visited Madīnah for the purpose of learning Islām and al-Qur'ān. Abū Hurairah, who is famous for narrating the largest number of *Aḥādīth* [sayings of the Prophet(s.a.w.)], was one of the *Aṣḥāb-uṣ-Ṣuffah.*

Masjid-un-Nabawī at Madīnah.

Two small rooms were attached to the Mosque to serve as *Ḥujrah,* the living quarters of the Prophet (s.a.w.) They were simple like the Mosque. and were covered in order to give privacy for living purposes. Upon completion of the Mosque, the Prophet (s.a.w.) moved to his *Ḥujrah* with his family.

This mosque is known as *Masjid-un-Nabawī* (the Mosque of the Prophet), and is the second holiest place for the Muslims. This was the place from which the Prophet (s.a.w.) laid the foundation of the first Islamic state. It became the central point of the whole Muslim community. It served as the educational, political, and social headquarter of the *Ummah,* from where evolved the whole system of the newly established community.

Besides being a place for worshipping Almighty Allāh, the mosque has a great social significance for the Muslims. It is an excellent platform where the Muslims have the opportunity to meet with other members of the community and learn about their welfare. Five times a day, congregational prayers keep the Muslims in touch with one another and conscious of each others' needs. They share the happiness and sorrow of one another.

As a gesture of great respect and goodwill, a family of Madīnah presented an extremely brilliant boy, Anas, to the Prophet (s.a.w.), so that he could assist him and also acquire knowledge from him. Reading and writing well at the age of ten, this boy was a pride for the whole family.

Rehabilitation of the displaced people was the most pressing need of the Muslims at that time. They had to be integrated into the local situation. To establish *Mawakhat* (brotherhood) between the *Anṣār* and the *Muhājirūn,* the Prophet (s.a.w.) convened a general meeting and suggested to the *Anṣār*: "Each one of you accept one *Muhājir* as his brother and take care of his needs." The *Anṣār* agreed to this suggestion wholeheartedly.

The Prophet (s.a.w.) himself matched one *Anṣār* with one *Muhājir*. The *Anṣār* happily accepted this brotherhood and each one of them offered half of his assets to his Makkan brother. Most of the *Anṣār* were farmers. They invited their fellow brothers to share the cropping of their land. They took this brotherhood not only in economic matters but also in all other spheres of life.

The brotherhood established by the Prophet (s.a.w.) turned out to be a permanent one. It continued even after the Makkan Muslims became economically independent. The *Anṣār* showed exemplary cooperation in helping their Muslim brothers, who had left all of their possessions behind. They did not leave any stone unturned in helping the Makkan Muslims to settle in their city. It was a unique phenomenon, unparalleled in history. The spirit which Prophet Muḥammad (s.a.w.) had infused in his followers, made them absolutely selfless and extremely generous.

The Makkan Muslims, on the other hand, did not seek to burden their noble brothers. They took only what was essential for their needs. They labored hard to make their living and to establish themselves. Some of them got engaged in trade, and the others began farming on the land owned by the *Ansar* under the system of sharecropping. When they became self-sufficient, they gratefully evacuated the properties of their *Anṣār* brothers.

Many of the *Muhājirūn* did not like to put even a little burden upon their brothers-in-faith. An *Anṣār,* Sa'd ibn Sabī, was one of the richest men of Madīnah. He said to his fellow-brother,'Abdur Raḥmān ibn 'Awf: "I will be very happy if you take half of my property." Unwilling to accept anything, 'Abdur Raḥmān answered: "May Allāh bless you, my brother. I do not want to take anything from you. Please show me the way to the market, so that I can make my fortune myself."

He went to the market and bought something on credit, and sold it off. Repeating the buying and selling several times during the day, he earned so much that not only could he return the loan but also had enough money left to buy food for himself. Several examples of this sort demonstrate that the Makkan Muslims behaved with the grace which matched the generosity of the *Anṣār*. They cared for the new relationship more than the blood relationship, but did not become a liability on their brothers.

During this period, the *Kuffār* in Makkah had not given up on the Prophet (s.a.w.). They took the successful migration of the Muslims to Madīnah very seriously. Soon, a delegation was on its way to Madīnah, demanding the locals to extradite the Prophet (s.a.w.) or face grave consequences. The delegation returned to Makkah without any success. This was an indication of trouble ahead. The Makkans were not ready to be silent observers of the victory of Islām in Madīnah.

Madīnah was a cosmopolitan city. The two big pagan tribes that were settled there were al-'Aws and al-Khazraj, who had continual battles between them. A number of people belonging to these tribes had embraced Islām and had invited the Prophet (s.a.w.) to their city. Many members of these tribes were still pagans. Besides them, a significant number of Jewish people, known as Banū Isrāel, were settled there. There were also some Christians living in Madīnah. The inhabitants of the city were exhausted by the prolonged hostility between the tribes.

The non-Muslim population of the city observed the scene of the arrival of Prophet Muḥammad (s.a.w.) with great interest. They were astonished to see that the 'Aws and Khazraj tribes, who had been the worst enemies for decades, had joined hands like brothers in welcoming Muḥammad (s.a.w.). Seeing these people as one group was unbelievable for them. Some of the people became apprehensive about the newly founded unity between the people and the influence of the new religion in their city.

« الدِّينُ النَّصِيحَةُ » قُلْنَا : لِمَنْ ؟ قَالَ : « لِلَّهِ ،
وَلِكِتَابِهِ ، وَلِرَسُولِهِ ، وَلأَئِمَّةِ الْمُسْلِمِينَ
وَعَامَّتِهِمْ » .

Religion is sincerity! We said: To whom? He said: To Allah and His Book, and His Messenger, and to the leaders of the Muslims and their common folk.

It was related by Muslim.

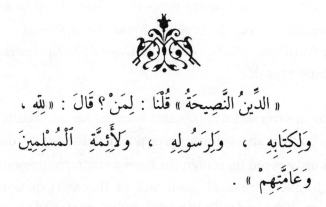

EXERCISE 4

A. Read each of the following statements carefully and circle T if the statement is true or F if it is false.

1. The first task of the Prophet (s.a.w.) in Madīnah was the establishment of a mosque. T/F
2. The Prophet (s.a.w.) himself participated in the construction of the Mosque. T/F
3. *Aṣḥāb-uṣ-Ṣuffah* were the rich people of Madīnah. T/F
4. Abū Hurairah narrated very few *Aḥādīth*. T/F
5. *Masjid-un-Nabawī* was the center of the Muslims in Madīnah. T/F
6. Congregational prayers helped in bringing the Muslims together. T/F
7. The *Anṣār* were mainly businessmen. T/F
8. The *Anṣār* and *Muhājirūn* set an excellent example of sincerity. T/F
9. The *Muhājirūn* liked to be burdens on the *Anṣār*. T/F
10. The *Kuffār* were disturbed about the success of Islām in Madīnah. T/F

B. Answer the following questions.

1. How was the *Masjid-un-Nabawī* built?
2. Who were the *Aṣḥāb-uṣ-Ṣuffah?*
3. How did the Prophet (s.a.w.) establish *Muwakhat* between the *Anṣār* and the *Muhājirūn?*

LESSON 5

THE PEACE AGREEMENT OF MADINAH

After building the Mosque, the Prophet (s.a.w.) concentrated upon the various problems faced by the community. He had to ensure the welfare and integrity of the Muslims. His wisdom and the generosity of the *Anṣār* had contributed a lot toward the rehabilitation of the refugees.

The *Anṣār* had whole-heartedly welcomed their Makkan brothers, but Madīnah was not a land of abundance. Most of the Muslims there were poor farmers. If the difficult task of the total integration of the community could not be accomplished, the risk was that after the beginning enthusiasm was over, the *Anṣār* might start taking the *Muhājirūn* as a burden on them.

More important than the economic aspects was the social condition of Madinah. The 'Aws and Khazraj tribes had a long history of deep differences among them, which had been set aside due to their new faith and the compassion they had found in the personality of the Prophet (s.a.w.). But just a small issue could ignite the old enmities and cause a havoc in the whole set-up of the newly founded community.

Then, there was the problem posed by those people of the 'Aws and Khazraj tribes, who had not accepted Islam. These people were concentrating their efforts on creating differences among the people and keeping the Muslim community at a distance from the other tribes living in and around Madīnah, especially the Jewish tribes. These were the 'People of the Book' and had been waiting for the arrival of the Prophet (s.a.w.) prophesied in their Holy Books.

Among them were Banū Qurayẓah, who lived in the nearby suburb of Fadak; Banū Qaynuqah, who lived within the city limits; and Banū Naḍīr, who lived nearby and in the locality of Khaybar, in the north of Madīnah. The pagans feared that if the Jewish tribes accepted Prophet Muḥammad (s.a.w.), the Muslims would become too strong to deal with.

The Jewish population was resented by the other tribes because it was affluent and it used to loan money to the people on interest, which resulted in the increase of their wealth and in the poverty of the others.

Looking at the circumstances, the Prophet (s.a.w.) found it essential to adopt measures to resolve the differences between the people and establish peace and solidarity on the soil of Madīnah. He had an aversion to war and had an earnest desire to make humankind live with one another amicably and happily.

The multi-religion atmosphere of Madīnah made it imperative that an atmosphere be created in which no one felt hurt. Islām is a religion that believes in human dignity and one of its principles is that there is no compulsion in religion. It was necessary that the Christians, Jews, and the pagans of the city had an equal opportunity to practice their religion with freedom and live together peacefully.

Prophet Muḥammad (s.a.w.) called a meeting of the Madīnan population, both Muslims and non-Muslims. In the meeting, he expressed his strong desire to establish peace and solidarity among the people of Madīnah. He suggested to ban inter-tribal feuds and unite against external aggression. All of the groups consented and a pact was signed among the various tribes, which ensured them complete freedom in practicing their religion and the security of their property.

This was the first political agreement between the Muslims and the non-Muslims. It proved that the Prophet (s.a.w.) did not want to convert anybody to Islām through any kind of pressure. It set up an example of forebearance and tolerance for the future Islamic states. It demonstrated that the objective of the Prophet (s.a.w.) was to spread Islam on earth through peaceful means and not through hurting anyone.

The agreement included a number of decisions which were written down so as to define the rights and obligations of the people of Madīnah. This was the first written constitution in the history of the world. Its important points were the following:

1. In case of an attack from the outside, all people of Madīnah would defend it together.
2. The Jewish tribes of Madīnah would not support the Quraysh of Makkah or their allies against the Muslims.
3. Nobody in Madīnah would be engaged in blocking anyone from performing his religious duties.
4. If two parties in Madīnah have some unsolvable disputes, then Prophet Muḥammad (s.a.w.) would be the deciding authority, whom no one would overrule.
5. All of the residents of Madīnah would participate equally in the expenses incurred in the case of an outside aggression.
6. The Muslims of Madīnah would consider the friends of the Jews as their friends, and the Jews would take the friends of the Muslims as their friends.
7. Any bloodshed in the city of Madīnah would be unlawful, and the support of the suppressed and weak would be the duty of everyone.

As the 'People of the Book', the Jewish people were closer to the Muslims than the pagans. Prophet Muḥammad (s.a.w.) had special consideration for them. His friendly gestures and his special affection towards the Judaic population indicated that he sought unity between the Muslims and the Jews. He probably thought that they would be the easiest to convince about the truth of Islām and would join the Muslim community.

After the peace agreement in Madīnah, the Prophet (s.a.w.) made an effort to persuade the neighboring tribes living in the suburbs of Madīnah to join him. He thought that such an agreement would eliminate bloodshed totally, within and outside Madīnah. For this purpose, he traveled to the Valley of Wuddān and included the tribe of Banū Hamzah ibn Bakr in the peace agreement.

Traveling to a few other places, he visited more tribes and was successful in getting a number of them to join the peace agreement of Madīnah. In this way, he concluded defense alliances with a number of neighboring tribes. Important among them were the tribes of Damra, Juḥaina, and Muzaina in the south, north, and west of Madīnah, respectively. Damra was the tribe to which Abū Dharr Ghiffārī, one of the earliest to convert to Islām, belonged.

These measures not only ensured the security of the Muslims but also helped in getting the religion of Islām to penetrate among the members of the allied tribes. ‘Amr ibn Umaiyyah al-Damirī became so faithful to the Prophet (s.a.w.) that even before his conversion to Islām, the Prophet (s.a.w.) sent him as his envoy to King Negus of Abyssinia.

All these steps were aimed at strengthening Islām and in developing the political, economic, and social aspects of the State of Madīnah.

EXERCISE 5

A. Read each of the following statements carefully and circle the correct answer: a, b, c, or d.

1. The city of Madīnah faced the issues of----
   a. the integration of the *Muhājirūn* in the new environment.
   b. the pre-Islamic differences between the tribes of the ‘Aws and Khazraj.
   c. the differences between the ‘People of the Book’ and the others.
   d. All of the above.

2. Prophet Muḥammad (s.a.w.) made efforts to-----
   a. create a peaceful atmosphere for everyone living in Madīnah.
   b. pressure all of the non-Muslims of Madīnah to accept Islām.
   c. establish peace for the Muslims only.
   d. None of the above.

B. Answer the following questions:
1. Why did the Prophet (s.a.w.) make a peace agreement in Madīnah?
2. How did the peace agreement help to spread Islām?
3. How did the Prophet (s.a.w.) treat the ‘People of the Book’?

LESSON 6

THE HYPOCRITES (*MUNĀFIQŪN*)

The Prophet (s.a.w.) began his efforts to ensure the happiness and welfare of all inhabitants of Madīnah from the very day of his arrival there. But before he could get enough time to fulfill his desire, the opposition gained momentum, both from inside and outside the city. A new group of people emerged, who outwardly professed to be the followers of the Prophet (s.a.w.), but were really against him and the religion of Islām. They are described in al-Qur'ān as hypocrites *(Munāfiqūn):*

وَمِنَ ٱلنَّاسِ مَن يَقُولُ ءَامَنَّا بِٱللَّهِ وَبِٱلْيَوْمِ ٱلْآخِرِ وَمَا هُم بِمُؤْمِنِينَ ﴿٨﴾

يُخَٰدِعُونَ ٱللَّهَ وَٱلَّذِينَ ءَامَنُوا۟ وَمَا يَخْدَعُونَ إِلَّآ أَنفُسَهُمْ وَمَا يَشْعُرُونَ ﴿٩﴾

Of the people, there are some who say:
'We believe in Allāh and the Last Day';
But they do not (really) believe.
They think they deceive Allāh and the believers;
But they do not deceive anyone except themselves,
And they do not realize it.

al-Baqarah
2: 8-9

'Abdullāh ibn Ubayy was the leader of the *Munāfiqūn*. Before the arrival of the Prophet (s.a.w.) in Madīnah, he had strong influence upon both the 'Aws and Khazraj tribes, and was almost an uncontested leader. The tribes of 'Aws and Khazraj had been weakened due to the battles between them, and a good number of their young men had been killed during the clashes.

To bring an end to the prolonged hostility and bloodshed, the seniors of the tribes were inclined to make 'Abdullāh ibn Ubayy their king, and had already prepared a crown for him. It was under these circumstances that the Prophet (s.a.w.) entered Madīnah. What a disappointment for a man who was sure to become the king of the city! The religion of Islām wiped out his influence and within a very short period, the Muslims emerged as the most powerful force in Madīnah.

Finding his ambitions lost, 'Abdullāh ibn Ubayy developed a strong disliking for the Prophet (s.a.w.) and his followers. The feelings of deprivation of his leadership prompted him to conspire against the Muslims and bring an end to their power in the city. Apparently, he became a friend of the Muslims, as it was easier for him to harm them in that position.

The Makkans came to know about the resistance of 'Abdullāh ibn Ubayy to the Prophet (s.a.w.). To exploit the situation, they sent a letter to 'Abdullāh, encouraging him to rebel against the Prophet (s.a.w.) and convey a threat to the inhabitants of Madīnah that failing in expulsion of the Prophet (s.a.w.) would result in a Makkan attack and the capture of their women and wealth.

This was a golden chance for 'Abdullāh ibn Ubayy. He gathered the pagans of Madīnah to persuade them to expel the Prophet (s.a.w.). The *Anṣār* heard about the meeting and got angry with 'Abdullāh ibn Ubayy and his compatriots. They had vowed that they would defend the Prophet (s.a.w.) against any danger, at any cost. Besides there were other people who had not accepted Islām until that time, but had appreciation for the Prophet (s.a.w.).

The Prophet (s.a.w.) was aversive to confrontations. He decided to go to the meeting himself and address the people. He told them that it was in their own interest to stick to the agreement reached with the Muslims. The people were convinced and refused to heed to the Makkan threat. This was a clear defeat of 'Abdullāh ibn Ubayy and the *Kuffār* of Makkah.

The refusal of the Madīnans did not stop the *Kuffār* from their conspiracies. An *Anṣār,* Sa'd ibn Mu'ādh, was on a visit to Ka'bah. Abū Jahl told him angrily: "You are supporting the people who have turned away from their religion. How do you expect us to protect you in Makkah?" Sa'd answered, "It is our right to visit Ka'bah, and we will never give up Islām. If you do injustice to us, we can stop your trade caravans going to Syria." Due to intervention of some people, Abū Jahl could not stop Sa'd from visiting Ka'bah.

Now, the Muslims were well-aware of the ambitions of the Makkans and their allies in Madīnah. "What should we do to ensure the security of the community in Madīnah?" they thought. They had to find some way to stop the Quraysh from their evil desires.

The best way was to exert economic pressure on the Quraysh. Makkah was a barren land and had no agriculture. It depended totally on commerce. The trade caravans brought them prosperity. The caravans going north to Syria were very important for them, as they were the means of exchanging goods brought from the Yemen with the northern areas, including Europe.

The caravans headed towards the north had to pass through routes which were close to Madīnah. Some of the tribes inhabiting these areas were allies with the Muslims. If the Muslims desired, they could stop the caravans and deprive the Quraysh of their commerce. They had a right to do that as they had been forced out of Makkah and their property had been confiscated.

They were justified if they decided to make raids on the Quraysh caravans and obtain their commodities as replacement for their losses. In fact, according to the tribal customs, they were in a state of war with the Quraysh. But the Prophet (s.a.w.) did not want to resort to such measures. He always focused upon peaceful means to resolve the issues.

« دَعْ مَا يَرِيبُكَ إِلَى مَا لَا يَرِيبُكَ » .

Leave that which makes you doubt
for that which does not make you doubt.

It was related by at-Tirmidhī and an- Nasā'ī ,
at-Tirmidhī saying that it was a good and sound Hadith.

EXERCISE 6

A. Read each of the following statements carefully and circle T if the statement is true or F if it is false.

1. Hypocrites are people who do not do what they say.	T/F
2. Almighty Allāh does not like hypocrisy.	T/F
3. The tribes of ʻAws and Khazraj were good friends before Islām.	T/F
4. ʻAbdullāh ibn Ubayy was a good man.	T/F
5. The Quraysh were prosperous because of their trade caravans.	T/F
6. The Prophet (s.a.w.) always avoided bloodshed.	T/F
7. The caravans to Syria were very important for the Makkans.	T/F
8. Makkah was an agricultural city.	T/F
9. The Makkans showed their cooperation to the Muslims.	T/F
10. The hypocrites conspired against the Muslims.	T/F

B. Answer the following questions.

1. What does al-Qur'ān say about the *Munāfiqūn?*
2. What position did ʻAbdullāh ibn Ubayy have in Madīnah before Islām?
3. What message did the Makkans send to the *Munāfiqūn* of Madīnah?

« لَا يُؤْمِنُ أَحَدُكُمْ حَتَّى يُحِبَّ لِأَخِيهِ مَا
يُحِبُّ لِنَفْسِهِ ».

None of you [truly] believes until he wishes for his brother what he wishes for himself.

It was related by al-Bukhārī and Muslim.

THE ORDER FOR SELF-DEFENSE: *JIHĀD*

It came to the knowledge of the Muslims that the Quraysh had intensified their efforts against the Muslims and were trying to obtain help from neighboring tribes to strengthen themselves to destroy the Islamic state of Madīnah. They also got the information that the Quraysh had increased their trade caravans in order to acquire more wealth to be used in preparation for war against the Muslims.

The Muslims had enough experience with the Quraysh and were aware of their hostility towards Islām. These pieces of information were sufficient for the Prophet (s.a.w.) to take some precautionary measures against the highly possible attack by the Makkans. He sent some *Ṣaḥābah* to gather information about the activities of the Quraysh and their caravans.

To deal with such an enemy, it was important to show some power so that it would be known that the Muslims were not in a weak position. But how to do that? The Prophet (s.a.w.) did not like bloodshed. He always chose peaceful means. He thought that the Muslims could use the economic weapon to prevent the Quraysh from starting military confrontation. He sent a message to the Quraysh: "If your caravans pass through Muslim territories, they will be raided."

This was the least he could do to make the Quraysh realize their mistake of continual confrontations with the Muslims. If they did not traverse the boundaries unlawfully, there was no danger of any clash.

There could not have been a more peaceful measure to deal with the hostile enemy, but the extremists among the Quraysh did not want to let the matter settle down so easily. They were on the lookout for an excuse for military encounter with the Muslims so that they could wipe them out.

As a result of boundary violations, the Muslim parties raided the Quraysh caravans and there were a few clashes. One such clash resulted in the death of a Makkan and the capture of two. ‘Abdullāh Jaḥsh, the leader of the raiding party, brought the two captives and the booty (wealth of the defeated party as a consequence of battle). The Prophet (s.a.w.) was angry with the killing of the Makkan. "I had instructed you to stop the Makkans and not to fight and kill them," he said.

Ibn Jaḥsh and the other members of the raiding party were scolded and punished by the Muslims. It was the holy month of Ramaḍān and fighting in it was not permitted. At that time, Allāh sent His *Waḥī*, directing the Muslims to fight if it was for the sake of Islām:

يَسْـَٔلُونَكَ عَنِ ٱلشَّهْرِ ٱلْحَرَامِ قِتَالٍ فِيهِ ۖ قُلْ قِتَالٌ فِيهِ كَبِيرٌ ۖ وَصَدٌّ عَن سَبِيلِ ٱللَّهِ وَكُفْرٌۢ بِهِۦ
وَٱلْمَسْجِدِ ٱلْحَرَامِ وَإِخْرَاجُ أَهْلِهِۦ مِنْهُ أَكْبَرُ عِندَ ٱللَّهِ ۚ وَٱلْفِتْنَةُ أَكْبَرُ مِنَ ٱلْقَتْلِ ۗ
وَلَا يَزَالُونَ يُقَـٰتِلُونَكُمْ حَتَّىٰ يَرُدُّوكُمْ عَن دِينِكُمْ إِنِ ٱسْتَطَـٰعُوا۟ ۚ وَمَن يَرْتَدِدْ مِنكُمْ
عَن دِينِهِۦ فَيَمُتْ وَهُوَ كَافِرٌ فَأُو۟لَـٰٓئِكَ حَبِطَتْ أَعْمَـٰلُهُمْ فِى ٱلدُّنْيَا وَٱلْـَٔاخِرَةِ ۖ وَأُو۟لَـٰٓئِكَ
أَصْحَـٰبُ ٱلنَّارِ ۖ هُمْ فِيهَا خَـٰلِدُونَ ﴿٢١٧﴾

> They ask you (O Muḥammad) with regard to warfare in the sacred month. Say,"Warfare in them is a grave offense, but graver is it in the sight of Allāh to prevent access to the Path of Allāh, to deny Him to prevent access to the Sacred Mosque, and drive out its members." Persecution is worse than killing. And they will not stop fighting against you until they turn you back from your faith, if they can. And if any of you turn back from their faith and die in disbelief, their work will bear no fruit in this life nor in the Hereafter. They will be the rightful owners of the Fire: they will abide in it.
>
> al-Baqarah
> 2:217

This *Waḥī* satisfied the Muslims regarding the incident as it was the permission from Allāh to fight if necessitated. The Prophet's reluctance to fight even for defensive purposes was only due to his fear of Allāh. He avoided fighting because his mission was to bring peace to the world.

Now, the events had taken a different turn. Almighty Allāh had ordered the Muslims not to avoid fighting if it was to safeguard their religion and defend themselves. Again, in another *Waḥī*, the Muslims were instructed to do *Jihād* where necessary:

وَقَٰتِلُوا۟ فِى سَبِيلِ ٱللَّهِ ٱلَّذِينَ يُقَٰتِلُونَكُمْ وَلَا تَعْتَدُوٓا۟ ۚ
إِنَّ ٱللَّهَ لَا يُحِبُّ ٱلْمُعْتَدِينَ ﴿١٩٠﴾

Fight in the Cause of Allāh,
Those who fight you,
But do not trangress limits;
For Allāh does not love trangressors.

al-Baqarah
2: 190

Jihād in Islām means struggle in the Way of Allāh. Its purpose is to support justice and the right cause. There are many forms of *Jihād*. Self-restrain or controlling oneself from wrong acts is *Jihād*. Helping the community by publications for the welfare of its members is another form of *Jihād*. Supporting the needy people is also *Jihād*. A Muslim can do *Jihād* through all or any of its forms throughout his life.

Jihād which involves fighting the enemy, is the duty of the Muslims whenever aggression comes from the enemy, and the religion of Islām and the Muslim community is in danger. The people who have been expelled from their homes or have been victimized by the enemy for believing in Allāh, should struggle for their rights and security. *Jihād* does not include offensive wars to expand the empire or to convert people to Islām by way of compulsion.

Islām is a religion which allows utmost freedom to the people to practice their beliefs. Muslims are supposed to live peacefully with believers of other religions. Al-Qur'ān has clearly stated that there is no compulsion in religion. It is the behavior of the Muslims which should be a model for humanity to follow, thus inviting the whole world to Islām.

Islām is not a religion of fantasies. It does not make demands from individuals which are beyond their powers and capabilities. Neither does it expect the people to be perfect. Its system takes care of the needs of the human beings beautifully, in accordance with their biological and psychological needs. It is the most rational of the systems that humanity has ever experienced.

It is a religion which naturally applies to individuals as well as to groups. It keeps a perfect balance between the rights and obligations of individuals and society. It is a religion based upon truth, which gives freedom and order to society in the most moral way.

Human interaction always involves friction of varying levels and kinds. Power and greed conquer men and drive them towards cruelty to others. War is a manifestation of such weaknesses of human beings, as they get satisfaction in subordinating others and sometimes, humiliating and punishing them.

To keep their self-dignity and to preserve their right to live in the way they choose, human beings are compelled to fight, even if they despise it. Al-Qur'ān condemns aggression strongly and absolutely forbids cruelty to others, but keeping the human nature in view, it permits Muslims to fight for their self-defense, and for safeguarding the Muslim society.

« قَالَ اللَّهُ : أَنْفِقْ يَا ابْنَ آدَمَ ، أُنْفِقْ عَلَيْكَ » .

Spend, O son of Adam, and I shall spend on you.

It was related by al-Bukhārī (also by Muslim).

EXERCISE 7

A. Read each of the following statements carefully and circle the correct answer: a, b, c, or d.

1. The Quraysh made war preparations against the Muslims by----
   a. seeking help from the neighboring tribes.
   b. increasing their trade caravans to obtain wealth to fight.
   c. none of the above.
   d. a and b.

2. The Prophet (s.a.w.) ordered his followers to stop the caravans of the Quraysh in order to-----
   a. kill the Makkans.
   b. obtain the wealth of the Makkans.
   c. press the Makkans to accept Islām.
   d. press the Makkans not to attack Madīnah.

3. *Jihād* means-----
   a. fighting in the way of Allāh.
   b. staying away from bad deeds.
   c. converting people to Islām by pressure.
   d. a and b.

B. Answer the following questions.

1. Why was the Prophet (s.a.w.) unhappy with 'Abdullāh ibn Jaḥsh?
2. Under what circumstances is fighting allowed for the Muslims?
3. Why do we call Islām the most rational system for the world?

LESSON 8

ESTABLISHMENT OF THE MUSLIM COMMUNITY

While resolving the political and economic problems of the community, the Prophet (s.a.w.) did not ignore its social needs. He made efforts to integrate the people from different tribes and different backgrounds, and foster amity among them. His own life-style, called *Sunnah*, was the best example for the Muslims to follow. 'Alī ibn Abū Ṭālib asked the Prophet (s.a.w.) about his *Sunnah* and the latter replied:

> Wisdom is my capital, reason the force of my religion, love my foundation, longing my vehicle, the remembrance of Allāh my constant pleasure, trust my treasure, knowledge my arm, patience my robe, and prayer is my supreme pleasure.

Almighty Allāh was gradually guiding His Messenger (s.a.w.), through *Waḥī,* about the development of the community and the organization of the Islamic state. He gave him rules and regulations of an Islamic society.

Ṣalāt, the five times a day prayer, had been made obligatory during the last year of the Makkan period. Now, *Ṣawm* (fasting), during the month of Ramaḍān, was ordained to be another pillar of Islām. It became obligatory for every healthy adult of the Muslim community. Almighty Allāh revealed:

يَـٰٓأَيُّهَا ٱلَّذِينَ ءَامَنُوا۟ كُتِبَ عَلَيْكُمُ ٱلصِّيَامُ كَمَا كُتِبَ عَلَى
ٱلَّذِينَ مِن قَبْلِكُمْ لَعَلَّكُمْ تَتَّقُونَ ﴿١٨٣﴾

> O believers! Fasting is prescribed for you as it was prescribed for the people before you, that you may have self-restraint.
>
> al-Baqarah
> 2: 183

Ṣawm is a means to bring Muslims close to Allāh. It is a manifestation of self-control, merely to please Allāh. During this period, it becomes a blessing for the whole community. It makes the people realize the sufferings of the people who do not have the means to provide sufficient food for themselves and their families. It encourages them to share the Bounties of Allāh with other Muslims.

After *Ṣawm*, the Almighty obligated the Muslims to pay *Zakāt* (regular charity). *Zakāt* is a certain amount of money that every Muslim, who has some assets, must distribute among the needy. The *Waḥī* states:

وَأَقِيمُوا۟ ٱلصَّلَوٰةَ وَءَاتُوا۟ ٱلزَّكَوٰةَ وَٱرْكَعُوا۟ مَعَ ٱلرَّٰكِعِينَ ﴿٤٣﴾

Establish *Ṣalāt,* give *Zakāt,* and lower your head in worship with those who lower their heads down in worship.

al-Baqarah
2: 43

There cannot be a greater system than the system of *Zakāt*, to take care of the needy people of the community. *Ṣadaqah* is general charity which is encouraged very much in Islām. *Zakāt,* however, is obligatory and it sets the minimum which a Muslim must pay. In al-Qur'ān. Allāh has frequently instructed the Muslims to establish *Ṣalāt, Zakāt,* and *Ṣawm.*

It did not take much time for the Muslim community to evolve itself as an integrated and disciplined group of people. Congregational prayers helped in bringing the Muslims together. After the prayers, the Muslims used to discuss their various problems and take counsel from one another.

Soon, the Prophet (s.a.w.) and his *Ṣaḥābah* felt the need for *Adhān* (the Call for *Ṣalāt*). It was important to remind the people about their duty of *Ṣalāt* during the day, when they were engaged in their various obligations.

A *Ṣaḥābī,* 'Abdullāh ibn Zubayr, told the Prophet (s.a.w.) that he had been taught the words of *Adhān* in a dream. 'Umar ibn al-Khaṭṭāb also reported that he had a similar dream. The Prophet (s.a.w.) took it as a guidance from Allāh and the words constituted the regular *Adhān.* Bilāl ibn Ribāḥ, who was from Abyssinia, had a beautiful voice. The Prophet (s.a.w.) appointed him the first *Mu'adhdhin* (Caller of *Ṣalāt*) in Islām.

The pleasurable sound of *Adhān* became the reminder of the Majesty of Allāh and a reminder for the Muslims to attend to their duty of *Ṣalāt:*

اَللهُ اَكْبَرُ - اَللهُ اَكْبَرُ - اَللهُ اَكْبَرُ
اَشْهَدُ اَنْ لَّا اِلٰهَ اِلَّا اللهُ ، اَشْهَدُ اَنْ لَّا اِلٰهَ اِلَّا اللهُ ،

أَشْهَدُ أَنَّ مُحَمَّدًا رَّسُولُ اللّٰهِ ، أَشْهَدُ أَنَّ مُحَمَّدًا رَّسُولُ اللّٰهِ ،
حَيَّ عَلَى الصَّلٰوةِ ، حَيَّ عَلَى الصَّلٰوةِ ،
حَيَّ عَلَى الْفَلَاحِ ، حَيَّ عَلَى الْفَلَاحِ ،
اللّٰهُ أَكْبَرُ ، اللّٰهُ أَكْبَرُ ،
لَا إِلٰهَ إِلَّا اللّٰهُ ۝

Allāh is Great, Allāh is Great.
Allāh is Great, Allāh is Great.
I bear witness that there is no God but Allāh.
I bear witness that there is no God but Allāh.
I bear witness that Muḥammad (s.a.w.) is the Messenger of Allāh.
I bear witness that Muḥammad (s.a.w.) is the Messenger of Allāh.
Come to prayer. Come to prayer
Come to your prosperity. Come to your prosperity.
Allāh is Great, Allāh is Great.
There is no God but Allāh.

Until that time, the *Qiblah* of the Muslims was al-Quds (Jerusalem), and they offered their *Ṣalāt* in its direction. Now, the *Waḥī* came from Allāh, ordering them to turn towards Ka'bah during *Ṣalāt.* The mosque in which this *Waḥī* came, is known as, *Masjid-ul-Qiblatayn* (the mosque of two directions). The *Waḥī* said:

قَدْ نَرَىٰ تَقَلُّبَ وَجْهِكَ فِي السَّمَاءِ ۖ فَلَنُوَلِّيَنَّكَ قِبْلَةً تَرْضَاهَا ۚ فَوَلِّ وَجْهَكَ شَطْرَ
الْمَسْجِدِ الْحَرَامِ ۚ وَحَيْثُ مَا كُنتُمْ فَوَلُّوا وُجُوهَكُمْ شَطْرَهُ ۗ وَإِنَّ الَّذِينَ أُوتُوا الْكِتَابَ
لَيَعْلَمُونَ أَنَّهُ الْحَقُّ مِن رَّبِّهِمْ ۗ وَمَا اللَّهُ بِغَافِلٍ عَمَّا يَعْمَلُونَ ﴿١٤٤﴾

We see turning your face to the heavens: Now, shall We turn you to a Qiblah which will please you? Then turn your face in the direction of the Sacred Mosque. Wherever you are, turn your face in that direction. The People of the Book know well that it is the truth from their Lord, nor is Allāh unaware of what they do.

al-Baqarah
2: 144

When the Jewish people and the pagans mocked the Muslims over the change in *Qiblah,* another *Waḥī* came to satisfy the Muslims:

* سَيَقُولُ السُّفَهَاءُ مِنَ النَّاسِ مَا وَلَّاهُمْ عَن قِبْلَتِهِمُ الَّتِي كَانُوا عَلَيْهَا ۚ قُل لِّلَّهِ
الْمَشْرِقُ وَالْمَغْرِبُ ۚ يَهْدِي مَن يَشَاءُ إِلَىٰ صِرَاطٍ مُّسْتَقِيمٍ ﴿١٤٢﴾

> Some foolish people will ask, "What caused them to change their old orientation?" Say: "To Allāh belongs the East as well as the West. He guides unto His straight path whomsoever He wills."
>
> al-Baqarah
> 2: 142

With astonishing speed, the Muslims gave up their old habits under the guidance of Prophet Muḥammad (s.a.w.). They became extremely disciplined, always ready to listen to their leader and follow him immediately.

Almighty Allāh guided the Muslims that to succeed in this world and in the *Ākhirah*, they must have their absolute faith and confidence in the Creator and must not go to fortune-tellers. The fortune-tellers used to take advantage of peoples' ignorance by telling them about the future. Al-Qur'ān specifically stated that only Almighty Allāh is Master of the future and nobody else has any power over peoples' destiny. In addition to it, the *Waḥī* made reference to the other three evils of the Arab society: *al-Khamr* (drinking), *al-Maiser* (gambling), and *al-Anṣāb* (idol-worshipping).

يَا أَيُّهَا الَّذِينَ آمَنُوا إِنَّمَا الْخَمْرُ وَالْمَيْسِرُ وَالْأَنصَابُ وَالْأَزْلَامُ رِجْسٌ مِّنْ
عَمَلِ الشَّيْطَانِ فَاجْتَنِبُوهُ لَعَلَّكُمْ تُفْلِحُونَ ﴿٩٠﴾

> O you who believe! drinking, games of chance, idol-worshipping, and divining arrows are only Satan's filthy work. Stay away from them in order that you may succeed.
>
> al-Mā'idah
> 5: 90

Clearly, the four evils, drinking, gambling, idol-worshipping, and fortune-telling, were forbidden. As soon as the Muslims heard this order of Allāh, they broke their wine cups and bars, and gave up all these evils.

EXERCISE 8

A. Read each of the following statements carefully and circle T if the statement is true or F if it is false.

1. *Ṣawm* was made obligatory before the Prophet's *Hijrah.* T/F
2. *Ṣawm* is a blessing for the whole Muslim community. T/F
3. *Ṣawm* gives a realization of others' sufferings due to poverty. T/F
4. *Zakāt* is to be given to the well-to-do members of the family. T/F
5. There is no fixed amount to be paid as *Zakāt.* T/F
6. Bilāl was the first *Muadhdhin* of Islām. T/F
7. Al-Quds was the first *Qiblah* of the Muslims. T/F
8. Gambling is an evil which is forbidden in Islām. T/F
9. Drinking was forbidden before the Prophet's *Hijrah* to Madīnah. T/F
10. Allāh is the Master of the East as well as the West. T/F

B. Answer the following questions.

1. Which three pillars of Islām are repeatedly mentioned in al-Qur'ān?
2. Why did the Muslims change the direction of *Qiblah*?
3. What does al-Qur'ān say about drinking, gambling and idol-worshipping?

« مِنْ حُسْنِ إِسْلَامِ الْمَرْءِ تَرْكُهُ مَا لَا يَعْنِيهِ » .

Part of someone's being a good Muslim is his leaving alone that which does not concern him.

A good Hadith which was related by at-Tirmidhī and others in this form.

LESSON 9

THE MIRACLE AT BADR
2 A.H

A caravan of Makkans led by Abū Sufyān was on its way back from Syria. Besides other commodities, it had war materials to be used against the Muslims. Everyone knew that the Muslims were not interested in bloodshed and violence, but Abū Sufyān, who was a staunch enemy of the Muslims, took this time as an opportunity to incite the Makkans. After passing safely through the route controlled by the Muslims, he sent a message to the Quraysh.

The message conveyed the fear that his men and commodities were in severe danger against a Muslim attack and he needed immediate military help to protect his caravan. This instigation was enough for the Makkans. All of the brave notables of Makkah were out to protect their trade. Without any delay, Abū Jahl set off with an army of one thousand soldiers, many hundreds of camels and horses, and a lot of arms.

Upon hearing about the army of the enemy, the Prophet (s.a.w.) consulted his *Ṣaḥābah.* Most of them were poor people. The *Anṣār* were simple farmers and the *Muhājirūn* were still struggling to establish themselves on the new soil. There was no way that they could prepare for a full-fledged battle with the Quraysh.

But the Quraysh were coming and the Muslims could not be silent observers of their might. They could not let them destroy their newly founded community. The Prophet (s.a.w.) told his *Ṣaḥābah:* "The Quraysh have sent their best men to fight you. What do you think we should do?" After Abū Bakr and 'Umar had given their views, al-Miqdād ibn 'Amr expressed his opinion in the following words:

> O Messenger of Allāh! move forward towards what Allāh has guided you. We are with you. We shall never say 'no' to you as the Jews had said to Mūsā, 'Go alone with your Lord and accompany Him in fighting for us, while we remain here and wait for your return.'

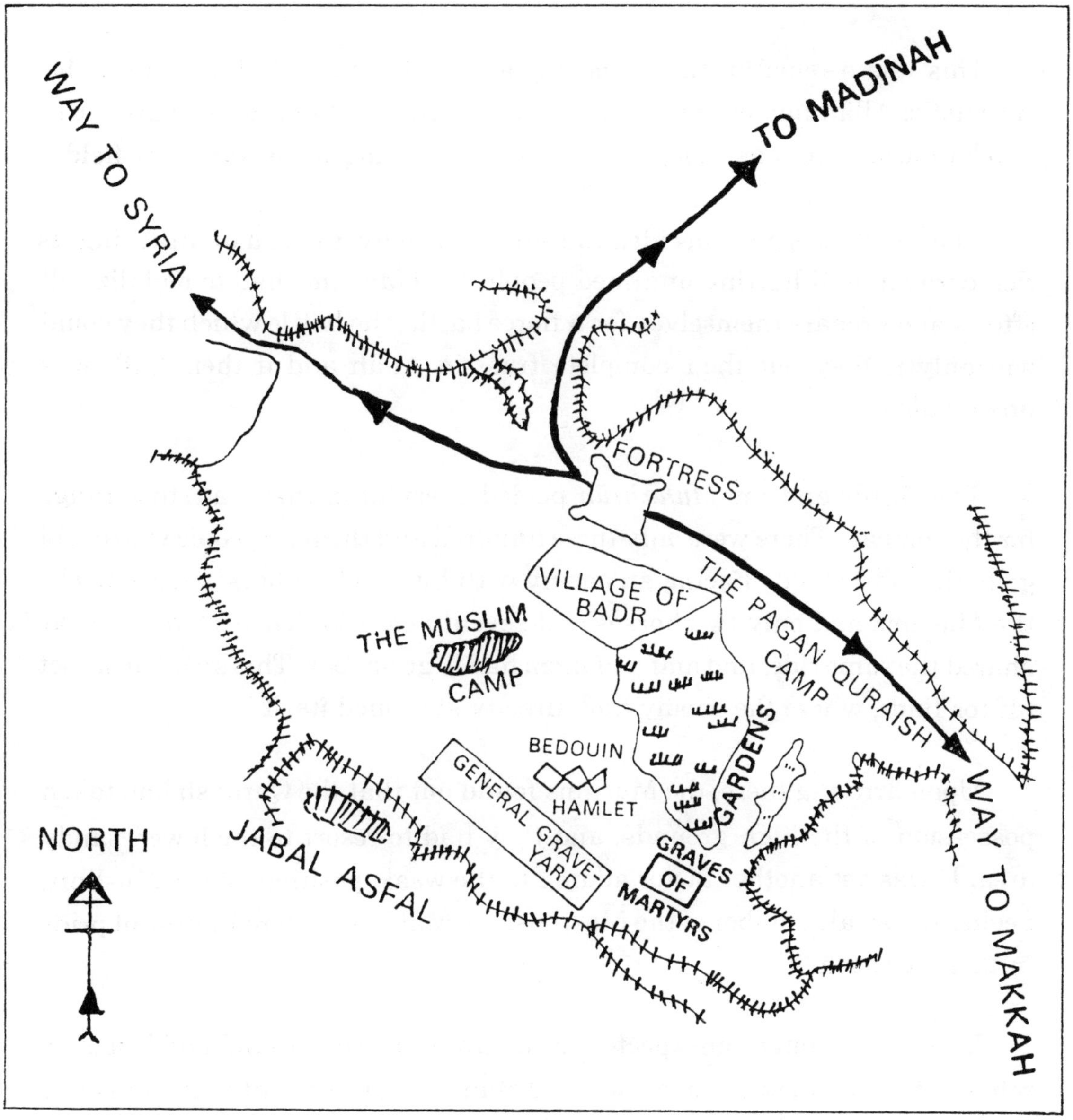

The Battlefield of Badr.

> Rather, we say, 'Go forth, you and your Lord, to fight, for we are joining you in this fight.'

The Prophet (s.a.w.) wanted to hear the comments from the *Anṣār*. After a brief period of quietness, the leader of *Anṣār*, Sa'd ibn Mu'ādh said:

> O Messenger of Allāh! We have believed in you, and we have witnessed that you have brought truth to us. We have promised to obey you. Go ahead with whatever you decide, for we are with you.

This was a relief for the Prophet (s.a.w.). He said: "Go forward and be optimistic; Allāh has promised me one of the two---either the caravan or the Makkan army. It is as though I see the enemy lying prostrate in the field."

The Prophet (s.a.w.) decided to fight the enemy, instead of attacking its rich caravan and hurting unarmed people. The Muslims had to mobilize all efforts and prepare themselves for a fierce battle, the battle which they could win only if they put their complete trust in Allāh and if their faith was unshakable.

The *Anṣār* and the *Muhājirūn* pooled everything they had to arrange for the combat. There were only three hundred and thirteen people who could go to the battle-field. Facing an enemy with hundreds of horses and camels, the Muslims had only two horses and seventy camels. Three or four people shared the same ride, and many of them had to go on foot. This small army set off for Badr, where the enemy had already stationed itself.

Upon arriving there, the Muslims found out that the Quraysh had taken possession of the high grounds, and they had to resort to the lower, sandy area. It was yet another factor adding to the weak position of the Muslims. Seeing the small number of the Muslims, the Makkans uttered words of pride in their strength.

The night brought unexpected rain, hardening the ground and bringing relief to the Muslims. From all worldly standards, the defeat of the Muslims was imminent, as their number and their supplies were no match to those of the enemy. But they stood firm to fight for the true cause.

It was a unique demonstration of the Muslims' faith in Allāh and His Prophet (s.a.w.). All this was to confirm their trust in the Prophet and to strengthen his position. None of them was seriously concerned about the result of the battle or his safety.

Sa'd ibn Mu'ādh suggested to make a booth to protect the Prophet (s.a.w.) and arrange for his safe return to Madīnah for the sake of the remaining Muslims in case of the Muslims' defeat. It was a superb example of trust and sincerity.

It was the morning of Friday, the seventeenth of Ramaḍān, and the second year of *Hijrah*. In spite of the pride in their army and supplies, the *Kuffār* planned the battle carefully. They were aware of the fearlessness and the passion of the Muslims for the sake of their faith. They thought that in case of an open combat, there was a possibility of their noblemen being attacked in the beginning. They preferred to start with a customary duel.

Al-Aswad al-Makhzūmī came to the ranks of the Quraysh, and sprang towards the Muslims. The Prophet's uncle, Hamzah ibn Abdul Muṭṭalib, struck him twice with his sword and brought him dead on the ground. No sooner had al-Aswad fallen down, than 'Utbah ibn Rabīah, with his brother, Shaybah, and his son, al-Waleed, came forward and challenged the Muslims. Three youth from the *Anṣār* went out to fight them.

Recognizing the youth, the Quraysh said: "We do not want to fight you. We will fight our own tribesmen, the pure-blooded Quraysh." One of them shouted at the top of his voice: "O Muḥammad! send out the people of our own tribe." Hearing this, the Prophet (s.a.w.) sent Ḥamzah ibn al-Muṭṭalib, 'Alī ibn Abū Ṭālib, and 'Ubaydah ibn Ḥārith.

The duel began and within a few minutes, Ḥamzah had finished Shaybah and 'Alī had killed Waleed. Then both of them turned toward 'Ubaydah to assist him in fighting the remaining enemy.

The army of the *Kuffār* advanced and a general collision of the two forces began. The Prophet (s.a.w.) organized the Muslim ranks. Looking over the army of the enemy, some of the Muslims became apprehensive. The Prophet (s.a.w.) went to his booth and made a passionate prayer to Allāh:

> O Allāh! the arrogant Quraysh have come to demonstrate to the world that Your Prophet is a liar. Give us assistance as You promised. O Allāh! if this small army of the Muslims is defeated, who will worship You? Grant us victory, O Allāh!

When the Prophet (s.a.w.) finished his prayer, his face was radiant. He told the Muslims that he had seen the vision of victory and they should enter the field fearlessly, by putting their faith absolutely in the Almighty.

The Muslims had nothing to lose. If they could crush the *Kuffār*, they were victorious. If they were killed in the battle-field, they would be *Shuhadā'* (sing.: *Shaheed,* one who lays down his life for the Sake of Allāh, and is sure to get a reward of *Jannah*). All of them fought bravely, killing numerous *Kuffār*. Allāh sent invisible help for them and they defeated the enemy.

An *Anṣār* youth, Mu'ādh ibn 'Umrū, attacked and injured Abū Jahl. Abū Jahl's son, 'Ikrimah, came forward for his rescue, and cut Mu'ādh's hand from the shoulder. Mu'ādh continued fighting with the same injurious condition for the remaining period. Later, another *Anṣār* youth killed Abū Jahl.

The *Kuffār* began withdrawing from the field and the Muslim soldiers followed them to some distance. In their nervousness, they forgot to take the body of their leader, Abū Jahl. Many of the *Kuffār* were dead and seventy were taken as prisoners. In the Muslim ranks, only fourteen became *Shuhadā'*. Almighty Allāh had fulfilled His promise of victory to the Muslims. The Prophet (s.a.w.) and his followers thanked Allāh for His Blessing.

Al-Qur'ān says regarding this *Ghazwah* (a battle in which the Prophet himself participated):

إِذْ يُوحِي رَبُّكَ إِلَى ٱلْمَلَٰٓئِكَةِ أَنِّي مَعَكُمْ فَثَبِّتُوا۟ ٱلَّذِينَ ءَامَنُوا۟ ۚ سَأُلْقِي فِي
قُلُوبِ ٱلَّذِينَ كَفَرُوا۟ ٱلرُّعْبَ فَٱضْرِبُوا۟ فَوْقَ ٱلْأَعْنَاقِ وَٱضْرِبُوا۟ مِنْهُمْ كُلَّ بَنَانٍ ﴿١٢﴾

Your Lord revealed to the angels, He is with you and commanded them to give firmness to those who believe. He announced that He will cast terror in the hearts of those who disbelieve.

al-Anfāl
8: 12

This event is known as *Ghazwat-ul-Badr* (the Battle of Badr). It was the beginning of the establishment of Muslim power in Arabia. It founded an empire which provided a civilization to the world, which reached its glorious heights when Europe was still in the Dark Ages.

The captives of the battle were afraid of the worst treatment for the Muslims, as they were the same people who had turned them out of their homes. The Prophet (s.a.w.) treated them very kindly. None of them was killed. Those among them who could read, were asked to teach the Muslim children as a prize of their freedom, and others were freed after paying a certain amount of money.

« إِنَّ ٱللَّهَ تَجَاوَزَ لِي عَنْ أُمَّتِي الْخَطَأَ ، وَالنِّسْيَانَ ، وَمَا ٱسْتُكْرِهُوا عَلَيْهِ » .

Allah has pardoned for me my people for [their] mistakes and [their] forgetfulness and for what they have done under duress.

A good Hadith related by Ibn Mājah, al-Baihaqī, and others.

EXERCISE 9

A. Read each of the following statements carefully and circle the correct answer: a, b, c, or d.

1. Abū Sufyān asked for help from the Makkans because----
   a. the Muslims had attacked and robbed his caravan.
   b. he was expecting a Muslim attack while passing through their area.
   c. he was expecting an attack by other tribes.
   d. he wanted to incite the Makkans to begin a battle against the Muslims.

2. The leader of the *Anṣār* told the Prophet (s.a.w.):
   a. "We will fight on your side against the Quraysh."
   b. "We will not put our city in danger by fighting the Quraysh."
   c. "We believe in you and will obey you in every respect."
   d. a and c.

3. *Ghazwat-ul-Badr* was fought in the----
   a. first year after *Hijrah*.
   b. second year after *Hijrah*.
   c. third year after *Hijrah*.
   d. fourth year after *Hijrah*.

B. Answer the following questions.
1. Why did the Makkans send their army against the Muslims?
2. How did the Muslims prepare for the battle?
3. How did Prophet Muḥammad (s.a.w.) treat the prisoners of the battle?

LESSON 10

THE CHALLENGES

Just as he moved into the *Ḥujrah* attached to the Mosque, the Prophet's family arrived in Madīnah. It consisted of his wife, Sawdah, whom he had married after the death of Khadijah, and his two young daughters, Umm Kulthūm and Fātimah. His other two daughters were already married. Among them was Zainab, married to Abū al-'As, and Ruqayyah, married to 'Uthmān ibn 'Affān. Later, after the death of Ruqayyah, the Prophet (s.a.w.) married Umm Kulthūm to 'Uthmān.

Fāṭimah was the youngest daughter of the Prophet (s.a.w.) and was seven years old when her mother, Khadījah, departed from this world. She was very much attached to the Prophet (s.a.w.) and was very dear to him. A few months after the victory at Badr, 'Alī ibn Abū Ṭālib, who was about twenty years old at that time, requested the Prophet (s.a.w.) for his marriage to Fāṭimah.

No doubt, 'Alī was the most suitable among the youth for the Prophet's daughter. He was an excellent match for Fāṭimah. Both of them had been close to the Prophet (s.a.w.) and were extremely pious. The Prophet (s.a.w.) asked Fāṭimah for her opinion, and after her agreement, accepted 'Alī's proposal.

The simple marriage ceremony took place in *Masjid-un-Nabawī*. It did not include big feasts. Since both 'Alī and Fāṭimah were under the guardianship of the Prophet (s.a.w.) himself, naturally, he cared for the necessities of their household. He gave a few things to them, which were bought from the money which 'Alī had obtained after selling some of his possessions.

The things which Fāṭimah and 'Alī took to their new home on this happy occasion were two millstones, a water carrier, two earthen jars, and a leather mattress. Also, the Prophet (s.a.w.) gave Fāṭimah a bracelet which her mother had left for her. One can imagine the simplicity of this function which did not involve any display of wealth or extravagance as is customary today.

As the triumph of Badr strengthened the Muslims, it created resistance and fear among the *Munāfiqūn* and the tribes of Banū Qaynuqah in Madīnah. 'Abdullāh ibn Ubayy had not given up his hope to be the king of Madīnah. The victory of the Muslims was a shock for him. Since he had good relationships with the pagans as well as the Jewish population of Madīnah, it was easy for him to launch a campaign against the Muslims.

Although Prophet Muḥammad (s.a.w.) had made an agreement with the Jews ensuring their security as well as their religious freedom, they were skeptical of the Muslim power in Madīnah. Contrary to the Prophet's assumption, they did not like to be friendly with the Muslims. They thought of themselves as the 'Chosen People' and did not want to accept an Arab as a Prophet.

The ground was fertile for 'Abdullāh ibn Ubayy to exploit and to use it against the Muslims. The pagans of the 'Aws and Khazraj tribes were already under his influence. In order to gain more power and support in Madīnah and break the power of the Muslims, he incited the Jewish population against the Prophet (s.a.w.). Tension between the tribe of Banū Qaynuqah and the Muslims increased, resulting in many ugly happenings.

Ka'b ibn al-Ashraf was a well-known poet of Banū Qaynuqah. After the Makkan defeat at Badr, he composed powerful and passionate poetry against the Muslims, inciting the Quraysh to take revenge. For this purpose, he himself traveled to Makkah and personally recited the eulogies of the Makkans killed at Badr in the gatherings of the Makkan nobles.

Referring to the dead Makkans, he exclaimed: "Those were the nobles of Arabia, the kings of mankind. By God, if Muḥammad has killed these people, the interior of the earth is a better dwelling than the top of it." He did not return to Madīnah until he had made everyone in Makkah hear his poetry and had intensified the Makkans' feelings of revenge. After returning to Madīnah, he caused more anger among the Muslims by falsely accusing the Muslim women of misconduct.

In addition to all that, Banū Qaynuqah got involved in conspiracies to kill the Prophet (s.a.w.) and tried to carry on a number of plans. But Allāh saved

His Messenger (s.a.w.) to let him complete His Mission as He had saved him from the hands of the Makkans. The Muslims observed all these activities with patience and forebearance, as the Prophet (s.a.w.) had instructed them.

The case which precipitated the Muslim anger was the incident in which a Muslim woman was undressed in the market by a man of Banū Qaynuqah. The incident took two lives and compelled the Muslims to deal with the mischiefs of Banū Qaynuqah strongly. They had made the atmosphere of Madīnah terribly ugly and impossible to endure any longer.

Banū Qaynuqah had themselves broken the peace agreement with the Muslims and the latter had every right to deal with them so as to bring back a peaceful atmosphere. The Muslims blockaded their fortress for fifteen days and then let them leave the city with all of their belongings, including a lot of gold. They decided to go to the north and settle down near the valley of Khaybar. Some of them went further north, closer to Syria.

The Muslims had hardly finished their encounter with Banū Qaynuqah when they had to deal with Abū Sufyān, who invaded a village in the vicinity of Madīnah. He came with two hundred armed men in the darkness of night, killed two people, and destroyed many orchards. He had vowed to take revenge from the Prophet (s.a.w.) for the Makkan defeat at Badr, and this was his way of carrying out his vow. Banū al-Naḍīr, in the suburb of Madīnah , welcomed him and gave him assistance.

After the invasion, Abū Sufyān left the scene quickly. The angry Muslims tried to catch him but in vain. They returned after an unsuccessful chase. This event prompted the Muslims to take even stronger measures to check the Quraysh. They began guarding the trade route carefully so as not to let any Quraysh caravan pass through their territory.

Madīnah was surrounded by a complex situation of rivalries and revenges. As the fame of Islām in the whole of Arabia was increasing, the activities of its enemies, too, were expanding. The *Munāfiqūn* of Madīnah acted as catalysts to the tension between the Muslims and the pagans, the Jewish population of Madīnah, and the hostile Quraysh of Makkah.

All of these groups wanted to see the Muslims crushed and wiped out. They had cooperation among them, making plans to hit the Muslims. The *Munāfiqūn* did not leave any stone unturned to encourage the Makkans to attack Madīnah again, with their promise to help them in defeating the Muslims.

The defeat of Badr was a serious blow to the tribal prestige and honor of the Quraysh. The feelings of hurt, due to the insult they had suffered at the hands of the Muslims, and the traditional thoughts of revenge, had made their lives difficult. Their prestige in the whole of Arabia seemed to be at stake.

Ka'b ibn al-Ashraf had popularized passionate eulogies for the dead ones of Makkah. No day was passed when the streets of Makkah were not sounded with these eulogies and the mourning for the Makkans killed at Badr. There were talks of a second battle with the Muslims, which they were sure to win.

The wealth that Abū Sufyān had brought, was utilized to buy arms and horses for the battle. Poets were sent to the other tribes of Arabia to invite people to help the Quraysh. Consequently, the two big tribes of Banū Kināna and Banū Tihāma joined hands with the *Kuffār* of Makkah. A number of other tribes also cooperated with the Quraysh

Over and above all this, the pagans of Madīnah, the Jewish tribes and the *Munāfiqūn* continued to convey all kinds of useful information to the Quraysh for their benefit. All of them concentrated their efforts to help the Quraysh topple the Islamic community of Madīnah.

EXERCISE 10

A. Read each of the following statements carefully and circle the correct answer: a, b, c, or d.

1. The poet who played an important role in inciting the Makkans against the Muslims was-----
   a. ‘Abdullāh ibn Ubayy.
   b. Ka‘b ibn al Ashraf.
   c. Abū Jahl.
   d. Abū Sufyān.

2. Among the enemies of the Muslim community of Madīnah were --------
   a. the Quraysh of Makkah.
   b. the non-believers of Madīnah.
   c. the *Munāfiqūn* of Madīnah.
   d. All of the above.

B. Answer the following questions.

1. Which members of the Prophet's family joined him in Madīnah?
2. Why was ‘Alī the best match for the Prophet's daughter Fāṭimah?
3. How was the marriage ceremony of ‘Alī and Fāṭimah?
4. How did the Quraysh of Makkah prepare to attack the Muslims?

LESSON 11

THE UḤUD ENCOUNTER

3 A.H.

The Makkans made heavy preparations for one whole year to topple the state of Madīnah and bring an end to the success of the religion of Islām which had challenged their fore-fathers' customs and which had brought serious insult to their honor in the whole of Arabia. The feelings of revenge and the urge to win back their lost prestige prompted them to use all of their resources towards this end.

An army of three thousand well-equipped soldiers set off for Madīnah. The daughters and the wives of the nobles killed at Badr accompanied them, encouraging them and keeping their spirits high for the revenge of their loved ones. Poets recited inciting poetry throughout the way. When this army reached near Madīnah, the Prophet (s.a.w.) came to know about it.

He conducted a meeting of the *Ṣaḥābah* and sought their counsel. The leader of the *Munāfiqūn*, 'Abdullāh ibn Ubayy, was present in the meeting. He and his associates suggested to defend the city from inside, but the majority of *Ṣaḥābah* favored going out and fighting the enemy in the open. They thought that fighting on the soil of Madīnah involved risks to the safety of the city as the enemy had a large number of soldiers and a lot of equipment.

It was Friday when the enemy reached close to the border of Madīnah. After *Ṣalāt*, the Prophet (s.a.w.) delivered the *Khuṭbah* that the victory of the Muslims depended upon their careful preparation and their patient and steadfastness. Then he returned home, got armed and led the Muslim army out of Madīnah. The army consisted of only one thousand individuals, with a very limited supply of arms and food, but their faith in Allāh was very strong.

On the way, 'Abdullāh ibn Ubayy detached himself from the Muslim army with three hundred soldiers under his command. He said, "I am unhappy because the Prophet (s.a.w.) did not accept my suggestion." This was the most harmful and hypocritical step in lowering the morales of the Muslims and in helping the enemy to overpower them.

By the evening, they reached near the mountain of Uḥud, where the Quraysh had just arrived. Uḥud is about three miles from Madīnah. The Prophet (s.a.w.) asked the Muslims to take position on the front side of Mount Uḥud and arranged their ranks.

The Muslims were not afraid of fighting. They were eager to start *Jihād* for the sake of the true religion. Before they left Madīnah, the Prophet (s.a.w.) had not allowed many young boys to join the army because of their age. But two of them, Rafī' and Samrah, had managed to hide themselves and had traveled with them to Uḥud. When the Prophet (s.a.w.) noticed them, he told them to go back. At this, Rafī' stood on tiptoe to demonstrate that he was a grown up man. The Prophet (s.a.w.) allowed him to stay. But what should Samrah do? Being short, he could not do the same. "I am more powerful than Rafī'," he told the Prophet (s.a.w.). In wrestling, he showed that he was stronger than his friend. The Prophet (s.a.w.) allowed him to stay, too.

Observing the faith and bravery of the young boys, the Muslims were very much delighted. They said to one another,"The *Munāfiqūn* cannot harm us. Even our children are so enthusiastic to fight in the Cause of Allāh. We have nothing to worry about." All this was due to their unshakable trust in the Prophet (s.a.w.) and his leadership and their total faith in Allāh.

The Muslim army took position on the front of the mountain.Their backs were protected by the mountain, but on one of its sides was a strategic pass. The Prophet (s.a.w.) appointed fifty archers to guard the pass. Their job was to defend against the attack of the enemy from the rear through the pass. The Prophet (s.a.w.) ordered the archers: "Do not leave the pass under any circumstances, unless I, myself, call you to do so." While he ordered other soldiers not to start fighting until he told them to, the archers were instructed to attack the enemy as soon as they saw them. This was to prevent them from reaching the ranks of the main army of the Muslims. 'Abdullāh ibn Jubayr was appointed as the leader of the guarding party.

Abū Sufyān was the Commander of the Quraysh. His wife, Hind, whose father, 'Utbah, had been killed during the Badr encounter, was anxious for revenge. She was on the forefront to incite the Quraysh to attack the Muslims

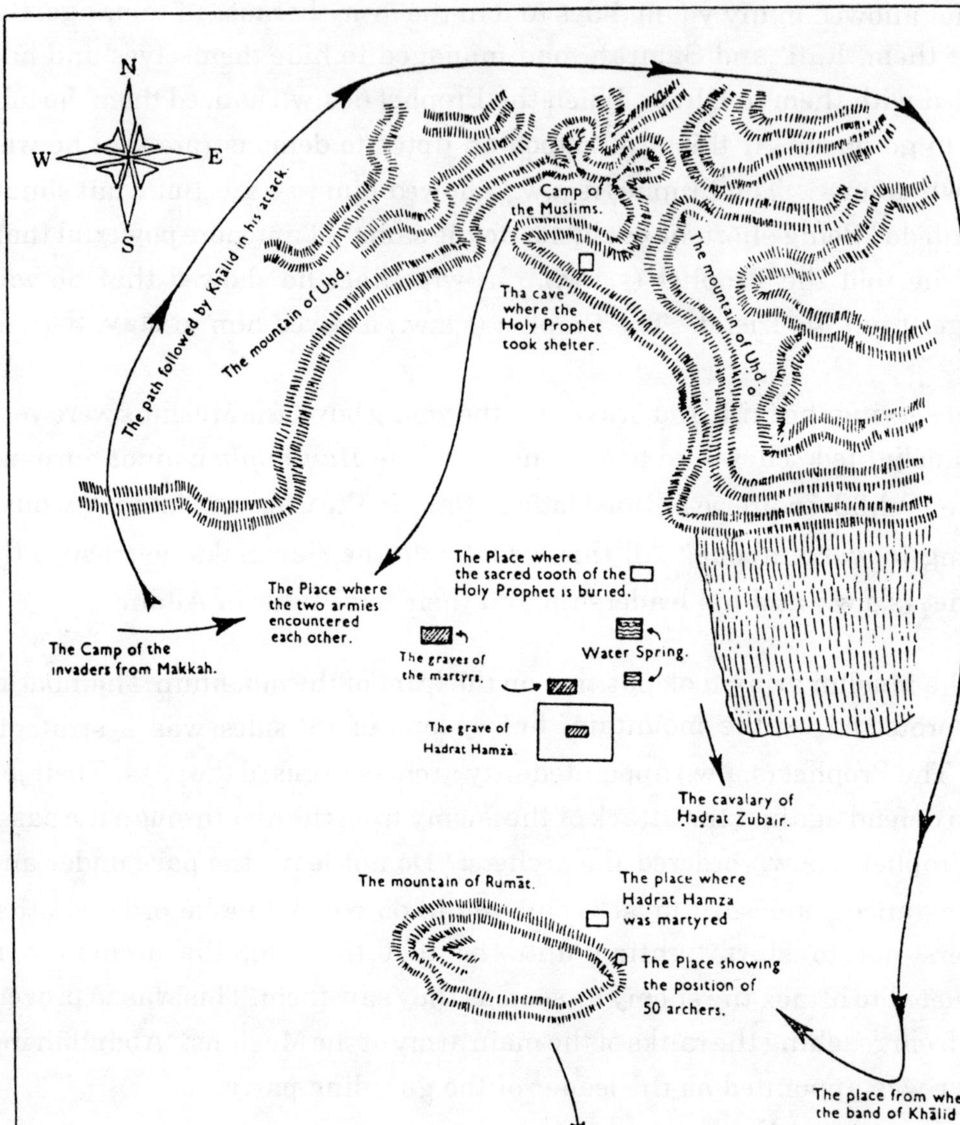

The Battlefield of Uḥud.

strongly and was the leader of the women who were singing eulogies and beating drums to arouse and encourage the Makkan soldiers. They were giving messages to their brave men:

We are the daughters of stars in the sky.
We walk over the carpets.
If you proceed with bravery,
You will be close to us.
If you show your back to the battlefield,
We will dissociate from you.

In the midst of the drum-beating and the battle-cry by the Quraysh and the Muslims' remembrance of Allāh and His help, the battle began. Less than seven hundred Muslims were facing three thousand *Kuffār*. Soon, the scene of Badr seemed to be repeated and the Quraysh were running backward. Then, they turned their backs to the battlefield and began to withdraw. Their women, who were singing, abandoned their drums and joined the fleeing men.

Abū Dunajah had the Prophet's sword in his hands, and was piercing through the ranks of the Quraysh. Suddenly, he saw a woman in front of him. She was Hind, the staunch enemy of the Muslims. Abū Dujanah raised his sword and was about to kill her, when he changed his mind. He brought his sword down. His anger had been overpowered by his grace and dignity. Killing a woman was of little honor to him. He let her go, knowing that she would spare no moment in her efforts to crush the Muslims.

Undoubtedly, the Muslims had won the battle. The field was almost empty and the Muslims were pursuing the *Kuffār*, but the battle was not completely over yet. At this critical moment, the archers, guarding the strategic pass, could not resist the desire to join the victorious Muslims in following the enemy. They began leaving their posts. 'Abdullāh ibn Jubayr tried to stop them, but in vain. Gradually, all of them left, except 'Abdullāh and a few others.

Khālid ibn Waleed, who was famous for his bravery, had not accepted Islām until that time. He was the commander of the Makkan cavalry. He spotted the guards leaving their positions and decided to attack the Muslims from the rear of the mountains. He took a detour with two hundred soldiers, and attacked the pass. The few remaining guards were caught in confusion and were killed, and Khālid occupied the mountain side. He signaled to the fleeing Quraysh to attack the Muslims again.

The Muslims were unprepared for the rebound of the enemy and some of them were occupied with the booty left by the *Kuffār*. The second attack caught them by surprise and the victory began turning into defeat. Khālid's success gave new vigor to the enemy, and they fell upon the Muslims with their swords and bows.

Everyone among the *Kuffār* sought to reach the Prophet (s.a.w.) and kill him, in order to get the appreciation from all of the *Kuffār*. An arrow of the enemy injured the Prophet (s.a.w.) and his teeth were broken. Seeing this, 'Ali ibn Abū Ṭālib rushed to the Prophet (s.a.w.) and gave him assistance. Simultaneously, Ṭalha ibn 'Ubaydullāh joined him, and together, they lifted the Prophet to his feet. While defending him from the enemy, they retreated to the mountain of Uḥud. Moments after this, many Muslims joined them, circling the Prophet (s.a.w.) and making a strong wall of defense between him and his bloodthirsty enemies.

A Muslim woman, Umm 'Amārah al-Anṣāriyah, had been busy since morning in the battlefield, supplying water to the soldiers. Upon seeing the Prophet (s.a.w.) in danger, she threw the jug of water, and drew her sword to join the protective shelter of the Prophet (s.a.w.). She continued shooting arrows at the enemy until she was injured by an enemy attack. Abū Dujānah became the shield of the Prophet (s.a.w.) by standing in front of him and exposing his back to the arrows of the enemy.

During this confusion, the news spread that the Prophet (s.a.w.) had been killed. This demoralized many Muslims and they lost the vigor to fight. One of them, Ka'b ibn Mālik, saw the Prophet (s.a.w.) alive and announced at the top of his voice that the Prophet (s.a.w.) was safe and sound. By that time, the enemy had inflicted injuries on the disappointed Muslims and had killed many of them.

On the side of the pass which Khālid ibn Waleed had occupied, 'Umar ibn al-Khaṭṭāb repulsed the attack and forced the enemy to retreat. When the

Muslims regained their vitality, the enemy began withdrawing from the field again. Finally, all of its soldiers retreated. The Muslims regained control of the battlefield but after heavy losses. Seventy of their men had become *Shuhadā'* (martyrs) and many were injured.

In this *Ghazwah,* many brave Muslims gave up their lives, protecting their belief and their brothers-in-faith. The Prophet's uncle, Ḥamzah ibn 'Abdul Muṭṭalib, was one of them. His death was celebrated among the *Kuffār.* The Muslims returned to Madīnah, sad on the loss of their loved ones, but happy on the safety of their Prophet (s.a.w.).

According to the peace agreement with the Muslims, the tribe of Banū Qurayzah, living in the suburb of Madīnah, should have helped the Muslims in the fight against the Quraysh, but it did not do so, and remained a spectator.

Among them was Mukhariq, a learned rabbi, who had recognized Prophet Muḥammad (s.a.w.) as the one prophesied by the religious books. He told his tribesmen: "It is incumbent upon you to help the Muslims because you have a defense pact with them." Nobody heeded to his advice. Finally, he decided to go alone. He fought along with the Muslims and died in the battlefield. When the Prophet (s.a.w.) came to know about him, he appreciated him very much and said that he was the best Jew.

« قَالَ اللّـهُ : يَسُـبُّ بَنُو آدَمَ الدَّهْـرَ ، وَأَنَـا الدَّهْـرُ، بِيَدي اللَّيْلُ والنَّهارُ » .

Sons of Adam inveigh against [the vicissitudes of] Time, and I am Time, in My hand is the night and the day .

It was related by al-Bukhārī (also by Muslim).

EXERCISE 11

A. Read each of the following statements carefully and circle T if the statement is true or F if it is false.

1. The Makkans wanted to take revenge from the Muslims.	T/F
2. The Muslims decided to defend the city from inside.	T/F
3. 'Abdullāh ibn Ubayy left the Muslims because he was a *Munāfiq.*	T/F
4. Uḥud is fifty one miles from Madīnah.	T/F
5. The Muslim army consisted of three thousand soldiers.	T/F
6. The Muslims won the battle in its first phase.	T/F
7. Abū Jahl was the commander of the Makkan cavalry.	T/F
8. The Muslims paid a high price for the mistake of the archers.	T/F
9. Umm Amārah was a brave woman who fought in the battlefield.	T/F
10. 'Umar ibn al-Khaṭṭāb did not participate in this battle.	T/F

B. Answer the following questions.

1. Why were the Muslims not afraid of the power of the *Kuffār?*
2. What instructions did the Prophet (s.a.w.) give to the archers?
3. Why did the Muslims have heavy losses after their victory in the beginning?

« إنَّ مِمَّا أَدْرَكَ النَّاسُ مِنْ كَلامِ النُّبُوَّةِ
الأُولَى : إذَا لَمْ تَسْتَحِ فَاصْنَعْ مَا شِئْتَ » .

Among the words people obtained from the First Prophecy are: If you feel no shame, then do as you wish.

It was related by al-Bukhārī.

LESSON 12

OBEDIENCE OF ALLĀH IS NECESSARY FOR SUCCESS

In spite of the heavy casualties, the Muslims did not mourn their dead fellows as the *Kuffār* of Makkah had done after Badr. Thinking about the reward in the *Ākhirah* (Hereafter) pacified them when they remembered their loved ones slain in the battle. The presence of the Prophet (s.a.w.) among them was sufficient to give them pleasure.

"Your father is dead," one of the soldiers coming from Uḥud told a woman. Instead of mourning her father, the woman asked, "How is the Prophet?" Ignoring her response, the informant said, "Your brother was also killed." "But tell me how is the Prophet of Allāh?" the woman repeated her question anxiously. "Your husband, too, is dead." The informant continued to give the tragic news about her relatives.

"In the name of Allāh, will anyone tell me how is our Prophet?" saying these words, the woman rushed towards Uḥud and did not stop until she had seen the Prophet (s.a.w.) with her own eyes. "Thanks to Allāh," she said, "so long as you are safe, the grief of our relatives carries little meaning." This was the spirit of the Muslims after the losses they had suffered in the battle. After sometime, a *Waḥī* came from Allāh:

وَلَا تَحْسَبَنَّ ٱلَّذِينَ قُتِلُوا۟ فِى سَبِيلِ ٱللَّهِ

أَمْوَٰتًۢا ۚ بَلْ أَحْيَآءٌ عِندَ رَبِّهِمْ يُرْزَقُونَ ﴿١٦٩﴾

Think not of those people who are slain in the way of Allāh as dead; in fact, they are alive and receive their provision in the presence of their Lord.

Āl-e-'Imrān
3: 169

Another *Waḥī* told the Muslims not to lose heart by the events of the battle and not to be afraid of the future as the Master of Destiny is Allāh alone:

إِن يَنصُرۡكُمُ ٱللَّهُ فَلَا غَالِبَ لَكُمۡۖ وَإِن يَخۡذُلۡكُمۡ
فَمَن ذَا ٱلَّذِي يَنصُرُكُم مِّنۢ بَعۡدِهِۦۗ وَعَلَى ٱللَّهِ فَلۡيَتَوَكَّلِ
ٱلۡمُؤۡمِنُونَ ﴿١٦٠﴾

If Allāh is your Helper, none can overcome you; and if He withdraws His Support, who is there to help you? So, let the believers put their trust in Allāh.

Āl-e-'Imrān

3: 160

Although the battle had ended indecisively, the Muslims could claim their victory as the enemy had not been successful in its attempt to invade Madīnah and destroy the Muslim community. But the price they had paid for this battle was high. They had been deprived of many brave Muslims and the Makkans found it easy to propagate that they had defeated the Muslims and it was the beginning of their end.

"Might is right," was the principle of Arabian society as it has usually been in the world. Hearing about the Muslim losses affected the tribes around Madīnah and they began considering their alliance with the Quraysh instead of the Muslims of Madīnah.

The Muslim community had established itself within a very brief period, in spite of the challenges from the *Kuffār,* the *Munāfiqūn,* and the Jewish tribes. But now, all of the enemy groups were rejoicing the harm faced by the Muslims at Uḥud. The Muslims were challenged by opposing forces from within and outside Madīnah. They began guarding themselves carefully and keeping a watch over the affairs.

The lessons they had learned at the clash at Uḥud, led them to assess themselves and to concentrate more upon getting rid of their weaknesses. They recognized that what had turned the tide of the battle and changed their sure victory into a chaos, was their disobedience to the orders of the Prophet (s.a.w.). They also recognized that discipline and patience was essential for any victory over the *Kuffār*. It was the lack of these qualities that had led the archers to leave their posts. So, they knew that obedience to Allāh and His Messenger was the key to their victory, and the disobedience would bring them humiliation. Almighty Allāh has told us in the Glorious Qur'ān:

وَأَطِيعُواْ ٱللَّهَ وَٱلرَّسُولَ لَعَلَّكُمْ تُرْحَمُونَ ﴿١٣٢﴾

Obey Allah and obey His Messenger that you may find Mercy.
Āl-e-'Imrān
3: 132

The *Kuffār* were satisfied that Uḥud had removed the disgrace of defeat at Badr. But the Prophet (s.a.w.) was neither disheartened nor worried about the new events. He kept himself abreast of the developments and prepared for the recognition of the power of Islām. The informants would come and tell him about the raids which the enemies were planning on Madīnah and he would take the necessary measures.

It was the routine of the Prophet (s.a.w.) to send teachers to different places to teach Islām to the people. Some tribesmen from the suburbs of Madīnah requested him to send a few *Sahabah* to teach the principles of Islām to their people. The Prophet (s.a.w.) accompanied six of his learned *Ṣaḥābah*.

When the party reached the locality of the Hudayl tribe, the host tribesmen betrayed the Muslims to the Hudayl, who killed four of them and sold two of them to the Makkans. This treachery of the Hudayl saddened the Muslims.

In a similar incident, Abū Bara, representing the people of Najd, requested Prophet Muḥammad (s.a.w.) to send some teachers. Considering the recent happening, the Prophet (s.a.w.) rejected this request in the beginning. But when Abū Bara said: "I take these people in my personal protection," the Prophet (s.a.w.) agreed and sent seventy of his best *Ṣaḥābah* to Najd to spread Islām there.

When the delegates reached the area of Banū Āmir and Banū Sulaym, Āmir ibn Ṭufayal planned to get all of the Muslims killed. At first he asked the people of Banū Āmir, but they refused to kill the delegates whom Abū Bara had given protection. At this, Āmir ibn Ṭufayl persuaded other tribes to do this job. Some of them listened to him and killed all of the Muslims near the well of Maʻūnah. There were only two survivors. Kaʻb ibn Zayd was wounded but was assumed by the enemy to be dead. Āmir ibn Umayyah was set free by Āmir ibn Ṭufayl because of a vow by his mother to spare the life of a man.

The Muslims blamed Abū Bara because he had pressed upon the Prophet (s.a.w.) to send the teachers. But Abū Bara was not directly responsible for the murder and he had a neighborly pact of goodwill with Prophet Muḥammad (s.a.w.). On the other hand, Abū Bara was annoyed with Āmir ibn Umayyah, who had killed the two men who turned out to be his clients. The *Shahādah* of the delegates was an extremely bitter event for the Muslims, although they were sure that their fellows would have *Jannah* as their reward. At the same time, they had to arrange for the blood money as compensation, to be paid to Abū Bara for the killing of his two men by Āmir unintentionally.

After losing all of his companions, when Āmir was returning to Madīnah, he came across two men whom he mistook as belonging to the same group which had killed all of the Muslim scholars. Furious over the death of his companions, Āmir killed both of them. Upon arriving in Madīnah, he reported every event to the Prophet (s.a.w.), who was deeply grieved to hear about the death of his delegates. All of the *Ṣaḥābah* were extremely gloomy over this event.

قُلْتُ : يا رَسُولَ اللهِ، قُلْ لي في الإِسْلامِ
قَولاً لا أَسْأَلُ عنهُ أَحَداً غَيْرَكَ ، قال : « قُلْ :
آمَنْتُ بِاللهِ ، ثُمَّ اسْتَقِمْ » .

I said: O Messenger of Allah, tell me something about Islam which I can ask of no one but you. He said: Say: I believe in Allah — and thereafter be upright.

It was related by Muslim.

EXERCISE 12

A. Read each of the following statements carefully and circle the correct answer: a, b, c, or d.

1. The result of *Ghazwat-ul-Uḥud* was that----
   a. the Muslims had a clear victory.
   b. the Makkans had a clear victory.
   c. the Makkans could not defeat the Muslims but harmed them very much.
   d. None of the above.

2. In the field of Uḥud, the Muslims learned the lesson that ----
   a. they must overcome their weaknesses.
   b. they must be careful about the *Munāfiqūn.*
   c. they must obey Allāh and His Prophet (s.a.w.) completely.
   d. All of the above.

B. Answer the following questions.

1. How did the Muslims feel about their brothers who were the *Shuhadā'* of *Ghazwat-ul-Uḥud*?
2. What did the *Waḥī* tell the Muslims about those who fight for Allāh?
3. Why did the Prophet (s.a.w.) send his *Ṣaḥābah* to different parts of Arabia?

LESSON 13

PLOT AGAINST THE PROPHET (S.A.W.)

4 A.H.

After Uḥud, the balance between the Muslims and the *Kuffār* of Makkah seemed to be equal, but the enemies did not want to lose any chance to harm the Muslims. The incidents of the killing of the Muslims by the Hudayl tribe and then at the well of Ma'ūnah, provided them with a good opportunity to propagate and conspire more against the Muslims. They planned to attack Madīnah and, at the same time, create the circumstances of a civil war in the city. The tribe of Banū Naḍīr and the *Munāfiqūn* collaborated for this purpose.

As a part of the agreement between the tribes, Banū Naḍīr were supposed to give their share of blood money. The Prophet (s.a.w.) decided to go to them near Qubā' to remind them of their obligation. He took ten of his closest *Ṣaḥābah* and visited Banū Naḍīr. They promised to bring money but, at the same time, tried to implement their scheme to kill the Prophet (s.a.w.).

While he was leaning over the wall of a house, 'Amr ibn Jaḥsh climbed the upper floor of the house with a heavy stone in his hands, with the intention of letting it fall on the Prophet (s.a.w.). The Prophet (s.a.w.) noticed it and left the place immediately. Banū Naḍīr invited him again but he refused, saying that he did not trust them any more.

In spite of this, the Prophet (s.a.w.) had not given up hope for a compromise leading to peace in the area. He communicated to Banū Naḍīr that he was ready to come if they renewed the peace agreement with the Muslims. The Banū Naḍīr refused to renew the agreement and displayed open hostility against the Muslims. They were proud of their strong fortresses and were anticipating support from 'Abdullāh ibn Ubayy and his associate *Munāfiqūn*.

They thought that the Muslims were under a lot of pressure and it was a good time to fight them. It was not the first incidence of their violation of the agreement with the Muslims. A year ago, they had extended hospitality to Abū Sufyān when he had come to invade the territory of the Muslims.

Under these circumstances, it became inevitable for the Muslims to clash with Banū Naḍīr in self-defense. They were visible danger to the security of the city especially to the Muslim community. They besieged their fortresses. Instead of coming out to fight, Banū Naḍīr shut themselves in their dwellings. After some days, they asked for permission to leave the town with all their belongings. Since the Prophet (s.a.w.) always preferred peace, he agreed to let them leave with whatever they could take with them.

Before evacuation, the Banū Naḍīr destroyed their fortresses as much as possible so that they could not be useful to the Muslims. They went to the north of Madīnah and settled down in the vicinity of Khaybar. It was a grave mistake on their part to develop hostility with the Muslims, who were offering them every gesture of reconciliation and peace. The *Munāfiqūn* who had promised to help them did not show up. Al-Qur'ān refers to this event:

هُوَ ٱلَّذِىٓ أَخْرَجَ ٱلَّذِينَ كَفَرُوا۟ مِنْ أَهْلِ
ٱلْكِتَٰبِ مِن دِيَٰرِهِمْ لِأَوَّلِ ٱلْحَشْرِ ۚ مَا ظَنَنتُمْ أَن يَخْرُجُوا۟ ۖ
وَظَنُّوٓا۟ أَنَّهُم مَّانِعَتُهُمْ حُصُونُهُم مِّنَ ٱللَّهِ فَأَتَىٰهُمُ ٱللَّهُ مِنْ
حَيْثُ لَمْ يَحْتَسِبُوا۟ ۖ وَقَذَفَ فِى قُلُوبِهِمُ ٱلرُّعْبَ ۚ يُخْرِبُونَ بُيُوتَهُم
بِأَيْدِيهِمْ وَأَيْدِى ٱلْمُؤْمِنِينَ فَٱعْتَبِرُوا۟ يَٰٓأُو۟لِى ٱلْأَبْصَٰرِ ﴿٢﴾

It is He, Who got the unbelievers among the People of the Book from their homes at the first gathering (of the forces). Little did you think that they would get out; and they thought that their fortresses would defend them from Allāh.But (the Wrath of) Allāh came to them from quarters from which they little expected (it), and cast terror into their hearts, so that they destroyed their dwellings by their own hands and the hands of the Believers. So, take warning! O you, who have eyes to see.

al-Ḥashr
59: 2

This Āyah pointed out that if these people did not give up their wrong ways, they would suffer the same fate again. This prophesy was fulfilled during the days of 'Umar ibn al-Khaṭṭāb when they were again expelled from Khaybar and left for Syria.

After the evacuation of Banū Naḍīr, the *Munāfiqūn* limited their activities and Madīnah regained its peace. The fear of secret plans among the enemies living in the city no longer remained. This period was marked by tranquility and satisfaction on the part of both the *Anṣār* and the *Muhājirūn*. The *Muhājirūn* were relatively settled by this time and did not require the assistance of the *Anṣār*. It was a period of prosperity. But this peace for which the Muslims had paid a high price, could not continue for a long time.

At the end of *Ghazwat-ul-Uḥud,* in the previous year, Abū Sufyān had threatened the Muslims of his return to Badr the next year. The news came that he was heading towards Badr. His representative, Nu'aym, came to Madīnah to inform the Muslims about the huge army which the Makkans were organizing to give a decisive defeat to the Muslims.

Some of the Muslims felt apprehensive to go to Badr to combat the enemy. The Prophet, however, decided to go and fight. He reminded his followers to have faith in Allāh. At this, all reluctance on the part of the *Ṣaḥābah* disappeared and they got prepared to set out for Badr.

Prophet Muḥammad (s.a.w.) appointed a *Ṣaḥābī*, 'Abdullāh ibn 'Abdullāh, as the leader of Madīnah in his absence and the Muslim army marched to Badr. Abū Sufyān would not dare to begin fighting the Muslims as the morale of his soldiers was very low and they were really scared of the Muslims. Under the pretext of bad weather, he returned to Makkah without combat.

After waiting for eight days in their camps, the Muslims went back to Madīnah. This movement is called Badr the Second. It removed the unpleasant memory of the second phase of *Ghazwat-ul-Uḥud* and strengthened the Muslims. The Prophet (s.a.w) was content that another battle had been avoided. He never liked bloodshed.

EXERCISE 13

A. Read each of the following statements carefully and circle the correct answer: a, b, c, or d.

1. The effect of the tragic incidents at Ma'ūnah and other places was that----
   a. the Muslim power was weakened.
   b. the Muslims stopped preaching Islām.
   c. no new people accepted Islām.
   d. the Makkans were encouraged to create more trouble.

2. After dealing with Banū Naḍīr, Madīnah enjoyed a peaceful atmosphere because-----
   a. there were no conspiracies by the people of the city.
   b. the Makkans did not find many friends in Madīnah.
   c. the hypocrites limited their activities.
   d. All of the above.

B. Answer the following questions.

1. Why did Prophet Muḥammad (s.a.w.) lose his trust in Banū Naḍīr?
2. Why did Nu'aym come to Madīnah?
3. Why did Abū Sufyān return without fighting the Muslims?

THE ALLIED OPPOSITION

5 A.H.

The unsuccessful attempt of Abū Sufyān to banish the Muslims reduced the activity of the Quraysh against the Muslims but made the Judaic people more apprehensive about their future in Arabia. They had already distinguished themselves as a distinct religious group and were constantly clashing with the Christians. They hoped to overpower Christianity and gain strength in the whole area. Now, another monotheistic religion was on its way to popularity. Its triumph would be the weakening of the Jewish power and influence.

Those scholarly Jews who had real insight in their religion and had been exposed to Islām, had understood its truth and had become Muslims. But most of them remained obstinate and refused to accept Prophet Muḥammad (s.a.w.) as the prophet who had been foretold in their Scriptures.

Banū Naḍīr had been expelled from the city for breaking the peace agreement and was making preparations to fight the Muslims. They had settled themselves in and around the town of Khaybar. They did not lose any time to conspire against the Muslims. It was not an easy time for the Prophet (s.a.w.). An organized campaign was going on to create disturbance within and outside Madīnah, and concentrated efforts were being made to produce general dissatisfaction against the Prophet (s.a.w.) and his followers.

During this difficult time, while dealing with all kinds of opposition forces, the Prophet (s.a.w.) did not neglect his mission of disseminating the light of Islām. For this purpose, he organized many groups of learned Muslims and sent them to different areas of Arabia. As mentioned before, the enemy took advantage of this and made treacherous plans to invite the Muslim preachers and to kill them.

The enemies of Islām were always in search of ways to insult and condemn the Prophet (s.a.w.). They thought if they could prove fault with al-Qur'ān, the people might give up the religion expounded by it. They began a movement of mispronouncing al-Qur'ān to change its meanings and to distort its teachings. There was also an increase in satirical poems against the Muslims aimed at inciting the enemies.

It was the best time for the leaders of Banū Naḍīr to take advantage of this hostile atmosphere against the Muslims. They made vigorous efforts to involve the whole of Arabia in attacking the Muslims.

When they approached the leaders of Makkah for this purpose, they were asked by the Quraysh: "You are the first people of the Scripture, and have the knowledge of our differences with Muḥammad. Is our religion best or that of his?" The Banū Naḍīr answered that the religion of the Makkans was far superior to what Muḥammad (s.a.w.) preached. One wonders how could they say this! They were the followers of Prophet Mūsā (p.b.u.h.), who had directed them to wipe out idol-worshipping absolutely. How could they prefer the pagan Makkans to Prophet Muḥammad (s.a.w.) who preached the worship of One God and condemned the man-made idols?

The Quraysh were delighted over the answer of Banū Naḍīr and collaborated with them. Large scale preparations began to crush the Muslims. The Makkans and the Banū Naḍīr contributed generously to the war-fund. All of the tribes of Arabia were approached in this campaign. It seemed as if the whole Arabia stood united to destroy Islām. Almost all of the tribes joined to form alliances (*Aḥzāb*) against Islām.

A huge army of twenty-four thousand soldiers, under the general command of Abū Sufyān, moved towards Makkah. Arabia had never seen such a mighty army before. At this time, Banū Quraẓah, who were next door neighbors to the Muslims and had a defense agreement with them, decided to join the enemy of the Muslims.

When the Muslims approached them and asked for support against the invading army, they flatly refused. Secretly, they had sent a message to the allied army that they would help them in defeating the Muslims after they came near Madīnah.

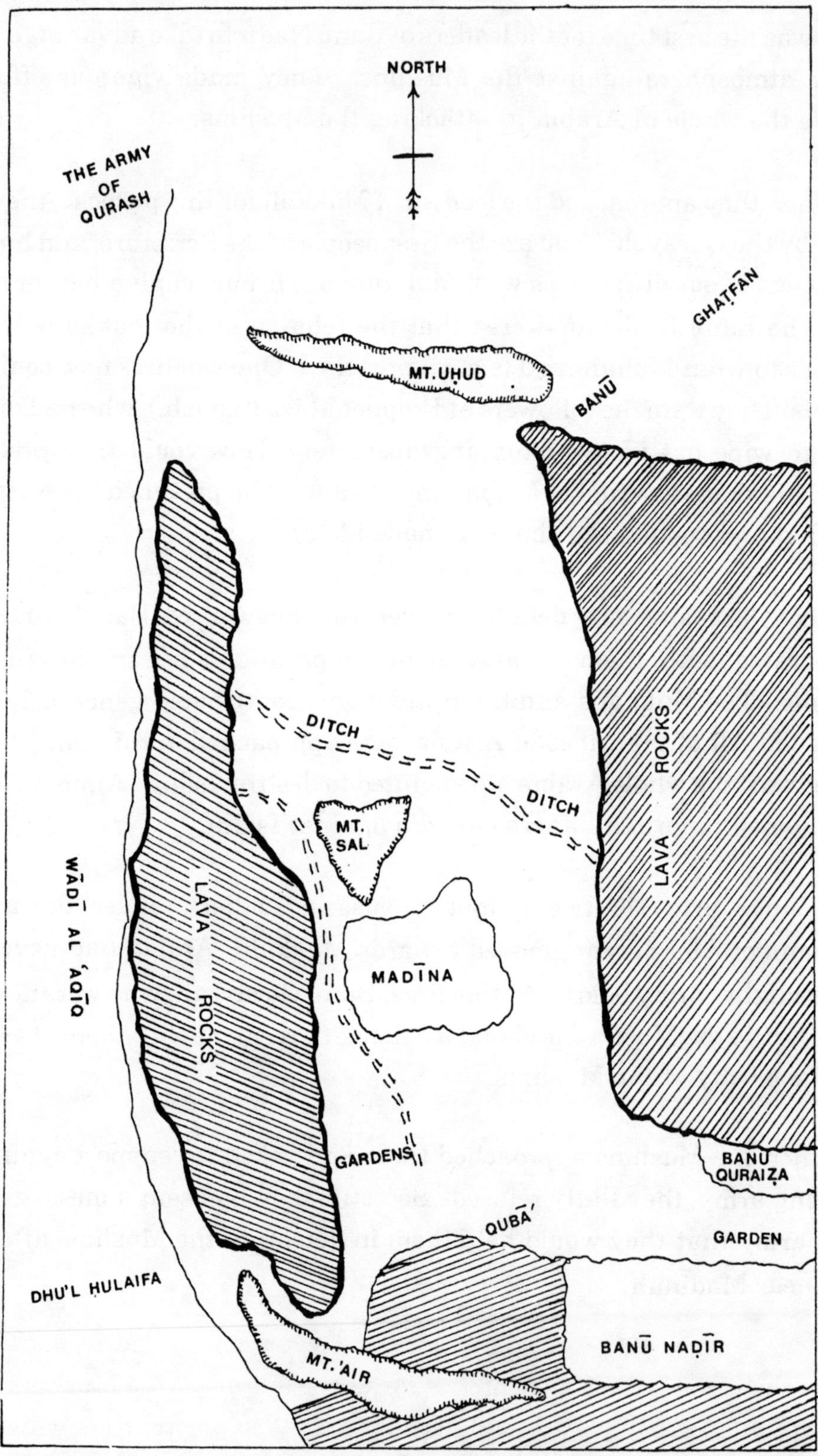

The Battlefield of Khandaq.

The Muslims were naturally shaken by this betrayal of Banū Qurayẓah. This had made Madīnah very vulnerable to the enemies as they had an open front to attack from the side of Banū Qurayẓah. Many of the inhabitants of Madīnah were in a panic. They were disappointed and disheartened. But the Prophet's calmness and his absolute trust in Allāh geve them consolation and the determination to defend themselves against the forces of ignorance.

Salmān al-Fārsī, a Muslim from Persia, suggested: "O Prophet of Allāh! the Persians defend their towns by digging trenches around them. Why don't we do the same?" This suggestion appealed to the Prophet (s.a.w.) and he made preparations for digging trenches on the front side of Madīnah at once.

The Muslims had very little time at their disposal, but with their hard labor, they began the task. The Prophet (s.a.w.) himself participated in the task just like an ordinary laborer and set an example of equality and humility.

Working ceaselessly and with little or no food, the Muslims faced the unbearable blasts of cold winds. Their enthusiasm for *Jihād* and trust in Allāh's Mercy was enough for them to pass through the trial patiently and bravely. They expressed their deep faith in the Creator with the following words:

> We start our work in the way of Allāh.
> How unfortunate it would be for us,
> If we worship anyone except Him!
> How nice and good is our Sustainer!
> How fine and excellent is our religion!

The allied forces reached the borders of Madīnah to crush the Muslims but were disappointed to see the trenches. This strategy of defense was unknown to them. They had no alternative but to lay siege to the city. They made many attempts on the trenches, but all of them were repulsed by the Muslims. Some of their bravest horsemen were able to take position on the inner side of the trench. 'Alī ibn Abū Ṭālib killed 'Amr Abd Wudd, the strongest of them, and the other horsemen ran away to save their lives.

Siege continued for many days and there was no end in sight. The enemy thought of other measures to lower the morale of the Muslims and to frighten them. They began sending their agents to the quarters which were close to the Muslim houses, where the women and children were staying with no arms and ammunition.

When one man of Banū Qurayẓah approached a house, a woman, Ṣafiyyah, an aunt of Prophet Muḥammad (s.a.w.), noticed him and struck him with a club. He died immediately. This created fear among the Banū Qurayẓah and they did not dare to go close to the Muslim houses.

The situation was getting worse and worse and the Muslims were running out of supplies, which were already quite limited. The *Munāfiqūn* (hypocrites) thought it was a good time for them to make fun of the Muslims. They said: "Their Allāh has promised them the treasures of Khusraw (Kisra) and Kaiser (Caesar), and look at their helplessness now." The Muslims did not lose heart. Their faith in Allāh could not be shaken. They were happy that they had a chance to demonstrate their steadfastness and trust in Allāh.

Undisturbed by all these developments, Prophet Muḥammad (s.a.w.) continued to make his decisions and direct the Muslims with the same calmness which was a characteristic of his personality.

As days passed, the morale of the Muslims lowered and the siege became tiring and bothersome. It was at this time that Almighty Allāh revealed the following *Waḥī*:

إِذْ جَآءُوكُم مِّن فَوْقِكُمْ وَمِنْ أَسْفَلَ مِنكُمْ وَإِذْ زَاغَتِ
ٱلْأَبْصَٰرُ وَبَلَغَتِ ٱلْقُلُوبُ ٱلْحَنَاجِرَ وَتَظُنُّونَ بِٱللَّهِ
ٱلظُّنُونَا۠ ﴿١٠﴾ هُنَالِكَ ٱبْتُلِىَ ٱلْمُؤْمِنُونَ وَزُلْزِلُوا۟ زِلْزَالًا
شَدِيدًا ﴿١١﴾ وَإِذْ يَقُولُ ٱلْمُنَٰفِقُونَ وَٱلَّذِينَ فِى قُلُوبِهِم
مَّرَضٌ مَّا وَعَدَنَا ٱللَّهُ وَرَسُولُهُۥٓ إِلَّا غُرُورًا ﴿١٢﴾ وَإِذْ قَالَت
طَّآئِفَةٌ مِّنْهُمْ يَٰٓأَهْلَ يَثْرِبَ لَا مُقَامَ لَكُمْ فَٱرْجِعُوا۟
وَيَسْتَـْٔذِنُ فَرِيقٌ مِّنْهُمُ ٱلنَّبِىَّ يَقُولُونَ إِنَّ بُيُوتَنَا عَوْرَةٌ وَمَا
هِىَ بِعَوْرَةٍ إِن يُرِيدُونَ إِلَّا فِرَارًا ﴿١٣﴾

> When they came upon you from above and from below you, and when eyes grew wild and hearts reached to the throats, and you imagined various (vain) thoughts about Allāh, in that situation were the believers tried, and were shaken with a mighty shock. And when the hypocrites, and those in whose hearts is a disease, were saying: "Allāh and His Messenger promised us nothing but delusion." And when a party of them said: "O folk of Yathrib! You cannot stand the attack, therefore, go back!" And certain of them sought permission from the Prophet (s.a.w.), saying: "Our homes lie open to the enemy," though they were not open, and they intended nothing but to run away.
>
> al-Aḥzāb
> 33:10-13

As dissension began appearing among some Muslim soldiers, very strong winds blew, accompanied by thunder and lightening. Extremely heavy rain started falling. The storm swept the tents of the enemies and with them, their food and other supplies were also blown away. All of the tribes began withdrawing from the field. Under the new situation, they were scared of the attack of the Muslims.

Abū Sufyān had no alternative but to order the Quraysh to leave the field. The next morning found the enemy completely wiped away. Not even a single soldier was left.

The scene was unbelievable. The pride of the mighty enemy had been shattered. The Almighty had demonstrated that the forces of ignorance and falsehood could never overpower the true believers. The Muslims returned to Madīnah with contentment and deep gratefulness to the Almighty, Who had saved His Messenger and his followers from the strongest army of the enemies. The Glorious Qur'ān mentions this battle in the following words:

يَٰٓأَيُّهَا ٱلَّذِينَ ءَامَنُوا۟
ٱذْكُرُوا۟ نِعْمَةَ ٱللَّهِ عَلَيْكُمْ إِذْ جَآءَتْكُمْ جُنُودٌ فَأَرْسَلْنَا عَلَيْهِمْ
رِيحًا وَجُنُودًا لَّمْ تَرَوْهَا ۚ وَكَانَ ٱللَّهُ بِمَا تَعْمَلُونَ بَصِيرًا ﴿٩﴾

O you who believe! Remember the Grace of Allāh on you when there came against you hosts (to overwhelm you). But We sent against them a hurricane and force that you could not see. And Allāh sees (clearly) all that you do.

al-Aḥzāb
33: 9

This event is known as Battle of Trench *(Ghazwat-ul-Khandaq),* or Battle of Alliances (*Ghazwat-ul-Aḥzāb*). After the battle, it was important to deal with the treacherous Banū Qurayẓah, who had stabbed the Muslims in their backs. They were besieged and were punished according to the Judaic Law, which they themselves had chosen.

EXERCISE 14

A. Read each of the following statements carefully and circle the correct answer: a, b, c, or d.

1. The fifth *Hijrah* year was a difficult period for the Prophet (s.a.w.) because-----
   a. the enemies were jointly trying to disturb the Muslim community.
   b. there was a famine in the area.
   c. the number of Muslims was reducing.
   d. the Muslims were fighting among themselves.

2. Banū Naḍīr told the Quraysh that-----
   a. the Muslims were better than the Makkans because they believed in One God.
   b. the Muslims were better than the Makkans because they followed the Book of Allāh.
   c. the Muslims and the Makkans were equal.
   d. the Makkans were better than the Muslims because their religion was superior.

B. Answer the following questions.

1. How did Banū Qurayẓah betray the Muslims?
2. How did Prophet Muḥammad (s.a.w.) react to the threat of the allied opposition?
3. What was the result of *Ghazwat-ul-Khandaq?*

LESSON 15

THE TREATY OF ḤUDAYBIYAH

6 A.H.

The victory over the united forces of opposition turned the situation in favor of the Muslims. They were not many in number and neither were they rich, but their strong faith and absolute obedience to Allāh had enabled them to defeat the most powerful army of the enemies. Allāh has told us in al-Qur'ān that if we help Him, He will help us. The encounter of Khaybar was an excellent example of the truth in the Words of Almighty Allāh.

It was the teaching and leadership of Prophet Muḥammad (s.a.w.) which had turned them into great Muslims and strengthened their will power. There was not a single moment when they had seen the Prophet (s.a.w.) tense or worried about the showdown of power on the part of the enemies. Instead, he kept on praying to the Almighty to help him and his followers against the bittesrest enemy of Islām. At the same time, he continually made efforts to raise the morale of the Muslims.

One day, the Prophet (s.a.w.) told his *Ṣaḥābah* that he had seen himself performing the *Ṭawāf* (circumambulation) of Ka'bah in a dream. During the *Ṭawāf*, he was unarmed and was not concerned about the enemy. It was an indication that he was performing *'Umrah* (short pilgrimage) in peaceful conditions. He conveyed the dream to *Ṣaḥābah* and began preparations to travel to Makkah to perform *'Umrah.*

There could not have been better news for the Muslims at that time. They were delighted. What a wonderful opportunity it was! Visiting the House of Allāh was an act of great pleasure for them. Especially, for the Makkan Muslims, it carried double charm. While visiting Ka'bah, they would also have the chance to see their homes.

It had been six years since they had left their homes. Although they loved Madīnah as their home city, sometimes they missed the place where they had grown up. Many of them still had very close relatives in Makkah, who had not become Muslims yet. "Maybe we would convince our relatives and bring them into the fold of Islām," they thought.

Under the leadership of the Prophet (s.a.w.), about fifteen hundred people, consisting of *Muhājirūn* as well as *Anṣār*, left Madīnah with the intention of performing *'Umrah,* in the Month of *Dhul Qa'dah.* They carried no arms and had no inclination to fight. Throughout the journey, they prayed to Allāh and thanked Him for saving them from the enemies and enabling them to travel to Makkah peacefully.

When the Quraysh heard about the Muslims approaching Makkah, they became alarmed. "How could the Muslims come to Makkah without arms after what the Makkans had done to them?" They did not believe that the Muslims desired to visit Makkah only for the purpose of pilgrimage.

They made war preparations and their soldiers blocked the route to Makkah. With arms and ammunition, they waited to stop the Muslims from entering Makkah. Upon knowing this, the Prophet (s.a.w.) decided to encamp at Ḥudaybiyah, a few miles from Makkah.

He sent his envoy to the Makkans with the message, "We have no intention to fight. We have come to perform *'Umrah* only and will return after performing it. Please allow us to enter Makkah peacefully and visit the House of Allāh."

Still the Makkans did not remove their army from the borders of the city. Instead, they sent a delegation to negotiate. Many delegates were sent back and forth from both sides. The delegates of Quraysh told the Makkans that the Muslims had no desire to fight. They were very much impressed by the loyalty of the Muslims to the Prophet (s.a.w). One of them, Urwah ibn Mas'ūd, commented to the Quraysh:

> I have been to the kingdoms of Khusraw of Irān, Kaiser of Rome, and Negus of Abyssinia, but never have I seen a king among his people as Muḥammad among his companions. When he makes his ablutions, they would not let the water fall on the ground. They compete with one another in order to obtain that. They will not abandon him under any circumstances. Judge properly and do whatever you desire.

The Quraysh did not believe even their own delegates. They charged them of taking sides with the Muslims. Negotiations prolonged and they were not ready to allow the Muslims to enter Ka'bah. Finally, the Prophet (s.a.w.) sent his son-in-law, 'Uthmān ibn 'Affān, who enjoyed respect among the Quraysh because of his family, most of which was still in Makkah.

Many days passed and 'Uthmān did not return. "What is the reason? Have the Quraysh killed him?" The *Ṣaḥābah* got quite perturbed. Sitting under a date tree, they gave *Bai'ah* (oath) to the Prophet (s.a.w.) that they would not hesitate in giving up their lives for the sake of Islām, if the situation demanded that. Every Muslim was eager to fight in the Way of Allāh and become *Shaheed* (martyr). The *Kuffār* heard about this and were convinced that attacking Muslims was of no use.

Finally, 'Uthmān returned safely and brought the message of Quraysh that they did not doubt the intentions of the Muslims any longer, but wanted them to return to Madīnah at that time and visit Makkah in the following year. They thought it as an insult for them to allow the Muslims to enter Makkah after they had made war preparations against them.

"Let us have a peace treaty," the Quraysh conveyed to the Muslims. They sent their envoy, Suhayl ibn 'Amr, to work out the terms of the treaty with the Muslims. He presented a number of conditions, some of which were not in favor of the Muslims. Many of the *Ṣaḥābah* opposed the acceptance of the treaty under the conditions which showed the Muslims to be in a weak position, but the Prophet (s.a.w.) accepted it.

He knew that the treaty would be a blessing for the Muslims. The terms of the treaty were the following:

1. The Prophet (s.a.w.) and his *Ṣaḥābah* would not visit Makkah this year but were allowed to return the next year and stay in Makkah only for three days.
2. There would be peace for ten years. The Makkans would be allowed to pass through the Muslim territory to go to Syria and the Muslims would be allowed to enter Makkah and Ṭā'if.
3. Any tribe which desired to make an alliance with the Muslims was free to do so; and likewise, any tribe which wanted to ally itself with the Quraysh, could do so.

4. Each of the parties would remain neutral in the battles of the other party with any third group.
5. If any Makkan took refuge with the Prophet (s.a.w.), he would be handed over to the Makkans, But if any Muslim took refuge in Makkah, he would not be handed over to the Muslims.

Immediately after the treaty, the tribe of Khuzā'ah decided to make an alliance with the Muslims and the tribe of Banū Bakr entered into an alliance with the Quraysh of Makkah. Abū Jandal ibn Suhayl, the son of the Makkan envoy, had been tortured by his own family for his acceptance of Islām. He came to the Prophet's camp in Ḥudaybiyah and sought asylum. According to the terms of the treaty, the Prophet (s.a.w.) had to hand him over to the Makkans.

The *Saḥābah* did not like their Muslim brother to be returned to *Kuffār*, but what could they do? The Prophet (s.a.w.) was extremely faithful to the treaty. He asked Abū Jandal to return to Makkah and advised him, "O Abū Jandal! have patience. Allāh will soon get you and others like you out of your sufferings."

When the Muslims were returning to Madīnah, Allāh revealed the *Sūrah al-Fatḥ* to His Prophet (s.a.w.):

إِنَّا فَتَحْنَا لَكَ فَتْحًا مُّبِينًا ﴿١﴾ لِّيَغْفِرَ لَكَ ٱللَّهُ مَا تَقَدَّمَ مِن ذَنۢبِكَ وَمَا تَأَخَّرَ وَيُتِمَّ نِعْمَتَهُۥ عَلَيْكَ وَيَهْدِيَكَ صِرَٰطًا مُّسْتَقِيمًا ﴿٢﴾

Indeed, We have given you a manifest victory. That Allāh may forgive you your faults of the past and that which is to come, and may perfect His Favor unto you, and may guide you on the Right Path.

al-Fatḥ

48: 1-2

EXERCISE 15

A. Read each of the following statements carefully and circle T if the statement is true or F if it is false.

1. In 6 A.H., the Prophet (s.a.w.) decided to attack the Makkans. T/F
2. A dream directed the Prophet (s.a.w.) to perform *'Umrah.* T/F
3. The Muslims felt very happy about visiting Makkah. T/F
4. The Quraysh welcomed the Muslims' visit to the sacred Ka'bah. T/F
5. The Muslims' love for the Prophet (s.a.w.) amazed the Makkan envoys. T/F
6. The Muslim did not enter Makkah because of the Makkan army. T/F
7. 'Urwah ibn Mas'ūd was a delegate of the Muslims. T/F
8. The *Ṣaḥābah* were anxious about 'Uthmān's delay in Makkah. T/F
9. All of the *Ṣaḥābah* were pleased with the peace treaty. T/F
10. *Sūrah al-Fatḥ* was revealed after the peace treaty at Ḥudaybiyah. T/F

B. Answer the following questions.
1. Why did the Prophet (s.a.w.) decide to perform *'Umrah?*
2. Why did the Muslims encamp at Ḥudaybiyah?
3. Why did the Prophet (s.a.w.) send Abū Jandal back to Makkah?

« لَمَّا قَضَى اللّهُ الْخَلْقَ ، كَتَبَ فِي كِتَابِهِ
على نَفْسِهِ ، فَهُوَ مَوْضُوعٌ عِنْدَهُ : إِنَّ رَحْمَتِي
تَغْلِبُ غَضَبِي » .

When Allah decreed the Creation He pledged Himself by writing in His book which is laid down with Him: My mercy prevails over My wrath.

It was related by Muslim (also by al-Bukhārī, an-Nasā'ī and Ibn Mājah).

LESSON 16

INVITATION TO OTHER KINGDOMS
7 A.H.

The Glorious Qur'ān says:

وَمَآ أَرۡسَلۡنَٰكَ إِلَّا رَحۡمَةٗ لِّلۡعَٰلَمِينَ ١٠٧

We have sent you (O Muḥammad) as a Mercy for all creatures.
al-Anbiyā'
21: 107

This Message clearly indicates that Allāh intended to make Islām a universal religion and had assigned His Last Messenger, Muḥammad (s.a.w.), the duty of guiding the whole world.

The peaceful atmosphere which the Treaty of Ḥudaybiyah had provided, helped the Prophet (s.a.w.) to concentrate more on his mission to spread Islām in the whole world. He addressed his *Ṣaḥābah* in the following words:

> O people! Allāh has sent me as a blessing to all mankind and now the time has come that you should spread this blessing to all corners of the world.

Then he selected some of the *Saḥābah* to act as his envoys and through them dispatched sealed letters to the neighboring Kings. The first envoy was sent to Caesar, the Emperor of Rome, which was the greatest Christian Empire. The letter of the Prophet (s.a.w.) contained the following:

> In the name of Allāh, the Merciful, the Compassionate. From Muḥammad ibn 'Abdullāh to Caesar, the Emperor of Byzantium. Peace be upon the rightly-guided. I call you to the religion of Islām. If you convert, you will be saved and Allāh will double your reward. If you do not convert, responsibility for the salvation of your subjects rests with you.
>
> O People of the Book! come to the Word that is common to both of us, that we worship none except Allāh, we do not associate anything with Him and that we do not take others as our Lords, besides Allāh. But they refuse, then say, 'Take note that we are Muslims'.

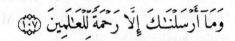

At that time, Emperor Caesar, was in Jerusalem, celebrating his victory over the Persians. The Prophet's envoy met with him, and after a brief introduction, presented him the letter sent by the Prophet (s.a.w.).

As was customary in those days, the letter was read aloud in the Emperor's court. Caesar became interested in Islām and sent for some Arabs to have more information about the new religion. Ironically, Abū Sufyān, the archenemy of Islām was there on a business trip. He was called by the royal court. The conversation which took place between them was as follows:

Caesar: What kind of a family does the Prophet belong to?

Abū Sufyān: He belongs to a noble family.

Caesar: Has there been any king in his family?

Abū Sufyān: No.

Caesar: Are the people who have accepted his religion, weak or strong?

Abū Sufyān: Most of them are weak.

Caesar: Are his followers on the increase or decrease?

Abū Sufyān: On the increase.

Caesar: Did he ever lie?

Abū Sufyān: No.

Caesar: Did he ever go back on his word?

Abū Sufyān: Not so far. We have made a treaty with him recently and we have yet to see if he abides by the new treaty.

Caesar: Have you ever fought him?

Abū Sufyān: Yes.

Caesar: Who has won the battle?

Abū Sufyān: Sometimes we have won and sometimes he.

Caesar: What does he preach?

Abū Sufyān: He preaches: "Worship only One God and join no partner with Him. Be pious, offer prayers, speak the truth, be kind to others, and give relations what is due to them."

Caesar was astonished to have such a positive response from a person who was a deadly enemy of Islām, and who had led many battles against it. "A person about whom even the enemy is unable to speak anything bad, cannot be a false person. Muḥammad must be a true prophet," Caesar thought. He did not speak frankly in front of his clergy who were very powerful and who were already resenting his hospitality to the Muslim envoy, but he could not help saying the following:

If you have spoken the truth, O Abū Sufyān, a day will come when his Kingdom will include my Empire. I wish I could go to Arabia and visit the Prophet.

Soon after that, the Prophet (s.a.w.) sent another envoy to Persia, to deliver his letter to Emperor Khusraw. The Emperor was too proud of his kingdom and his wealth. He became furious to see the letter and tore it into pieces. Then he ordered his governor of Yemen, named Bazan, to send soldiers to arrest the Prophet (s.a.w.). The governor obeyed him and sent two soldiers to Madīnah right away.

When the Prophet (s.a.w.) heard about the reaction of the Emperor to his letter, he said, "Allāh will scatter his empire into parts as he has torn my letter." When the soldiers of Bazan reached Madīnah, the Prophet (s.a.w.) told them that the Emperor whose orders they were following, had already been murdered by his son. The Prophet had been Divinely informed about the incident.

Hearing the news, the soldiers rushed back home and found the news to be true. Bazan was convinced about the truth of the Prophet (s.a.w.) and accepted Islām immediately.

Negus, the Christian King of Abyssinia, had a soft corner for the religion of Islām. He had given refuge to the Muslims when they were persecuted by the Makkans. He received the Prophet's envoy with great respect. After reading the letter, he accepted Islām and replied to the Prophet (s.a.w.) that he regretted his inability to present himself to the Prophet (s.a.w.).

The King of Egypt, Muqaddas, did not accept Islām, but replied to the letter of the Prophet (s.a.w.) respectfully and returned his envoy with some precious gifts. The Prophet's letter to the King of Egypt is preserved in the Topkapi Museum in Turkey.

It was surprising to the people that the Prophet (s.a.w.) could send letters of invitation to the greatest empires of the world from the small city state of Madīnah. But they observed the miracles of the conquest of the Persian Capital by the Muslims within five years, and within seven years, the conquest of Egypt by the Muslim general, 'Umar ibn al-'Āṣ. These victories of the Muslims were unparalleled in the entire history of mankind. All of the neighboring countries included in the Islamic State, contributed very much in the spread of Islām throughout the world. Now there are more than one billion Muslims in the world.

Like Egypt, Rome, Persia, and Abyssinia, Prophet Muḥammad (s.a.w.) continued sending envoys to various places. Some of the rulers welcomed his envoys and others were annoyed with them. Inside Arabia, many tribes accepted Islām in response to the Prophet's delegations. Among them were, the Ash'ar of Yemen and Abdul Qays of Baḥrain. The whole tribes of Ghiffār, Juḥniyah, and Ashja also embraced Islām.

All this success was in accordance with the promise by Almighty Allāh on the occasion of the agreement at Ḥudaybiyah. Apparently humiliating for the Muslims, this agreement proved to be a stepping stone for their later victories. It showed how wise the Prophet (s.a.w.) was in accepting the terms of the Makkans.

It helped tremendously in reducing tension between the Makkans and the Muslims. As communication opened between them, a lot of misunderstandings and misinformations were cleared. It became a lot easier for the Muslims to disseminate the teachings of Islām.

The state of Madīnah was still threatened by the Jews who had concentrated at Khaybar and had built strong forts there. After their failure in the Battle of Khandaq, they were looking for other means and opportunities to take revenge upon the Muslims. They sought help from Ghaṭafān tribe in attacking the Muslims.

The Prophet (s.a.w.) sent some Muslims to the Khaybar tribes, asking for a peace treaty. These tribes agreed in the beginning, but at the same time, continued treacherous activities against the Muslims. Their ally, Banū Ghaṭafān, raided a suburb of Madīnah and killed a Muslim. All of this created rage among the Muslims and they got ready to deal with the enemy.

About sixteen hundred Muslims, under the command of the Prophet (s.a.w.), set off for Khaybar. The people of the tribes confined themselves to their fortresses, which were besieged by the Muslims. For many days, the siege continued, with a few skirmishes.

Then the fortresses began falling. First, the fortress of Na'eem fell. The second fortress, Qāmoos, was the strongest. It seemed difficult to be conquered. The Prophet (s.a.w.) appointed 'Alī ibn Abū Ṭālib as the flag bearer of the Muslim army and sent him forward.

The Jews sent Marhab, who was among their strongest soldiers to face 'Alī. As soon as Marhab stepped up, 'Alī struck him with his sword and killed him. With his death, it became easier for the Muslims to capture the fortress.

Losing on every side, the Jewish tribes requested the Prophet (s.a.w.) for a truce. The Prophet had no desire to take the dwellings of the Jews. His aim was peace only. He granted the request gracefully and the battle ended. Observing the event of Khaybar, the Jewish tribes in other areas also entered into peace agreements with the Muslims. In this way, the hostility between the Jews and the Muslims came to an end.

أَنَّ رَجُلاً قَالَ لِلنَّبِيِّ صَلَّى اللهُ عَلَيْهِ وَسَلَّمَ : أَوْصِنِي ، قَالَ : « لَا تَغْضَبْ » ، فَرَدَّدَ مِرَاراً ، قَالَ : « لَا تَغْضَبْ » .

A man said to the Prophet (may the blessings and peace of Allah be upon him) :

Counsel me. He said: Do not become angry . The man repeated [his request] several times, and he said: Do not become angry.

It was related by al-Bukhārī.

EXERCISE 16

A. Read each of the following statements carefully and circle the correct answer: a, b, c, or d.

1. The Treaty of Ḥudaybiyah-----
   a. showed that the Muslims were weaker than the Makkans.
   b. was a defeat for the Muslims.
   c. was a victory for the Muslims.
   d. stopped the Muslims from visiting Ka‘bah forever.

2. Upon receiving the Prophet's envoy, Caesar-----
   a. listened to the letter of the Prophet (s.a.w.).
   b. became furious and tore the letter of the Prophet (s.a.w.).
   c. killed the Prophet's envoy.
   d. became a Muslim immediately.

B. Answer the following questions.
1. What does al-Qur'ān say about Prophet Muḥammad (s.a.w.)?
2. Why was Caesar surprised to hear the response of Abū Sufyān?
3. How did the Treaty of Ḥudaybiyah prove to be a blessing for the Muslims?

لَا يُؤْمِنُ أَحَدُكُمْ حَتَّى يَكُونَ هَوَاهُ تَبَعاً
لِمَا جِئْتُ بِهِ » .

None of you [truly] believes until his inclination is in accordance with what I have brought.

A good and sound Hadith which we have transmitted from Kitāb al-Ḥujja with a sound chain of authorities[2].

LESSON 17

RETURN TO MAKKAH

The Muslims in Abyssinia had been away from home for many years and could no longer resist the desire to be close to the Prophet (s.a.w.) and reunite with their Muslim brothers. Immediately after the victory in Khaybar, Madīnah welcomed Ja'far and other Muslims from Abyssinia enthusiastically. It was a great moment, the moment which confirmed that truth always overcomes falsehood.

Ja'far and his companions had migrated to Abyssinia after much suffering and persecution in Makkah. After about fourteen years, they were back in Arabia to live peacefully and happily with their relatives and friends.

Almost one year passed since the Treaty of Ḥudaybiyah. It was about the time when the Muslims were supposed to visit Makkah and perform *'Umrah.* Their longing for this sacred journey was increasing day by day. Finally, Prophet Muḥammad (s.a.w.) asked them to get ready for Makkah. He departed in the company of two thousand people.

According to the pact, the Quraysh had evacuated the town and moved to their tents in the surroundings of Makkah, so as to allow the Muslims to perform *'Umrah.* This time, the scene was totally different from the previous year. Instead of armed guards at the border, the city was almost empty.

The Muslims entered Makkah without resistance and began their religious rituals without any apprehension. Now, they realized their success at Ḥudaybiyah. They had observed how the peace agreement had been a blessing for them.

Many problems resulting from continual confrontations with the Makkans had been resolved. They had much more freedom to visit other tribes and preach the true faith. And now, they were at Ka'bah, with the consent of the Makkans. Those who were the staunch enemies of the Muslims, had evacuated the city for the Muslims to allow them to worship in the House of Allāh.

From their tents on the mountains and from the branches of the trees, the Makkans were spectators of the movements of the Muslims in their city. They were amazed to see the discipline and exemplary nobility of the Muslims. Many of them were their own fellows and relatives. How could they change like this? How did they give up their old habits? They had no answer to these questions, except that only a Divine Power could bring such a transformation. Were they right in their conversion to Islām? Was Muḥammad a true messenger of God? Puzzled by these questions, they watched how good the Muslims were to one another, and how efficient they were in obeying the commands of Allāh and His Messenger (s.a.w.).

"O Allāh! have Mercy on anyone performing this *'Umrah* today," Prophet Muḥammad (s.a.w.) prayed, showing the enemy a side of his spiritual strength. A *Ṣaḥābī,* 'Abdullāh, recited at the top of his voice: "There is no God but Allāh. He is always true to His Word. He gave victory to His Servant, who reinforced his army, who defeated all of the allies who had joined hands against his people."

When the Muslims repeated these words, the Makkans felt fearful. Many of them could not help thinking that they were surely on the wrong path. In their hearts, they were convinced about the truth of Islām. The favorable effect created on this occasion led to the conversion of many Makkans to Islām.

Khālid ibn Waleed, the greatest general of the Quraysh, said to his friends: "Anybody who has some intelligence can understand that Muḥammad is neither a poet nor a magician. What he says is truly the Word of God, the Lord of the universe. Everyone should follow him." Shocked at these comments, his fellows tried hard to convince him that he was wrong, but the more they argued, the greater was Khālid's belief in Islām.

Soon after that, the Muslims in Madīnah found Khālid among their ranks. After that, 'Amr ibn al-'Āṣ, another celebrated leader of the Makkan army, came within the fold of Islām. Then, 'Uthmān ibn Ṭalḥa, who was guardian of Ka'bah, joined the Muslims in Madīnah. The conversion of these leaders led to the conversion of many other Makkans.

This peaceful period in Madīnah could not continue for a long time. The Prophet (s.a.w.) found himself compelled to order an expedition to the northern border of Arabia. A nation which was ordered to respond fearlessly to aggression, could not remain silent when one of the envoys of the Prophet (s.a.w.), Ḥārith ibn 'Umayr, was murdered ruthlessly by the Governor of Buṣra, 'Umrū ibn Sharjeel, in Syria (Shā'm).

The Muslim army of 3,000 soldiers marched towards the northern border. The Romans were informed about the intentions of the Muslims. "How dare the Muslims challenge our men?" The Romans were furious. At once, they sent an army of one hundred thousand soldiers to Buṣra. The two armies stood face to face at a place called Mu'ṭah.

This was no match according to any standards. But what should the Muslims do? Would they return home without even trying to punish the aggressor? Would they be afraid of the mighty enemy? No, they would fight whatever the cost may be. Martyrdom for them was the noblest act. They preferred the reward of the *Ākhirah* to life in this world.

They plunged into the enemy ranks and fought courageously until three commanders were killed, one after another. Then Khālid ibn Waleed took charge of the Muslim army. As it was impossible to win the war, the best he could do was to withdraw the army without any further loss. Demonstrating his great skill, bravery, and intelligence, he withdrew the remaining soldiers from the field. This event is unparalleled in the history of warfare.

Although the battle was indecisive, the Roman army felt relieved when the Muslims withdrew. The courage and determination of the Muslims had taken them aback. How could a small army of 3,000 clash with the army of great Roman Empire?

The Muslims returned to Madīnah, remembering their brothers who had become *Shuhadā'* in the field of Mu'ṭah, but the impression they had made during their campaign in Syria was too deep. The tribes living on the northern border of Arabia had gotten a chance to witness the behavior of the Muslims. They had such an excellent impression of the soldiers of Islām that many people in the area accepted Islām.

Farwah ibn 'Amr was one of the Roman commanders and the chief of one of the tribes. "Nobody can deny that the Muslims are genuine and Islām is the true religion." Saying these words, he accepted Islām. The Emperor terminated his services and got him arrested. "I will reappoint you if you denounce Islām," he said to him. But Farwah refused to do so, and was executed by the Romans.

This execution did not stop the conversion of people to Islām. A large number of people in Syria and Irāq became Muslims after this incident. The true religion was revealed to be spread and not to be contained.

EXERCISE 17

A. Read each of the following statements carefully and circle T if the statement is true or F if it is false.

1. The Prophet (s.a.w.) performed *'Umrah* in the year after the truce. T/F
2. The Quraysh again resisted the Muslims' entry into Makkah. T/F
3. Ten thousand Muslims performed *'Umrah* with the Prophet. T/F
4. The Makkans were highly impressed with the Muslims' discipline. T/F
5. Ḥārith, the Prophet's envoy, was murdered in Egypt. T/F
6. Khālid showed great wisdom and courage in the field of Mu'ṭah. T/F
7. 'Amr ibn al-'Āṣ accepted Islām before the *Hijrah* of the Muslims. T/F
8. Fifty thousand Muslims fought the Romans in the field of Mu'ṭah. T/F
9. Many Makkans became Muslims after the *'Umrah* of the Prophet (s.a.w.). T/F
10. Three Muslim commanders became *Shuhadā'* at Mu'ṭah. T/F

B. Answer the following questions.

1. Why did the Muslims return from Abyssinia?
2. What did the Makkans do while the Muslims were performing *'Umrah?*
3. What effect did the Muslim army have upon the people of Syria?

LESSON 18

THE ISLAMIZATION OF MAKKAH

8 A.H.

The event of Mu'ṭah was an introduction of the true religion to Syria and the area around it. In fact, it opened doors for Islām in the whole northern area. But the foolish *Kuffār* could not see that. They assumed that due to their defeat in Mu'ṭah, the Muslims had been weakened.

"It is a good time for us to break the peace agreement and teach a lesson to the Muslims," they thought. Some of them, especially 'Ikrimah ibn Abū Jahl, encouraged Banū Bakr (the allies of the Quraysh) to attack Banū Khuzā'ah (the allies of the Muslims). In the darkness of night, Banū Bakr caught Banū Khuzā'ah by surprise, killing and injuring many people.

In panic, Banū Khuzā'ah ran to take shelter in the sacred Ka'bah. But here, too, they were mistreated by the Quraysh. "The Prophet of Islām would surely stand by his words and punish the Makkans," their leaders thought. They hastened to Madīnah to appeal to the Prophet (s.a.w).

How long could Prophet Muḥammad (s.a.w.) tolerate the mischiefs of the Makkans? Supporting attack against an ally of the Muslims was a clear violation of the Treaty of Ḥudaybiah. It meant that the Quraysh were again on the move to confront the Muslims. It was clear indication of their desire to fight.

The Prophet (s.a.w.) wanted to avoid bloodshed as much as possible. He sent a message to the Quraysh to accept any one of the following options or consider the peace agreement cancelled:

1. Withdraw support of Banū Bakr
2. Pay blood money as compensation to Banū Khuzā'ah.

The Quraysh responded that they would not agree to any one of the conditions of the Muslims and did not care about the truce with them. Now, there was no alternative left for the Prophet (s.a.w.) but to fight for the sake of truth and justice.

The wise men of Makkah, expecting some retaliation on the part of the Muslims, sent their most honored leader, Abū Sufyān, to Madīnah for a compromise. But the peace agreement had been broken, and there was no room for a compromise. The victimized tribe of Banū Khuzā'ah still had its representative in Madīnah. The Prophet (s.a.w.) had made his decision. The time had come to act.

Abū Sufyān's efforts proved fruitless and he returned to Makkah, worried about the fate of the city. He was unaware that the liberation of Makkah from the hands of the *Kuffār* was drawing closer and soon Makkah would be blessed by the conversion of its total population to Islām.

The Muslims had made no preparations for war, but the Prophet (s.a.w.) did not want to give time to the *Kuffār* to arm themselves and gather their allies. Without any delay, with absolute trust in Allāh's Mercy, he left Madīnah with two thousand Muslim soldiers and collected more of them on his way to Makkah. By the time they reached the borders of Makkah, the number of Muslim soldiers had increased to ten thousand.

'Abbās ibn 'Abdul Muṭṭalib, the Prophet's uncle in Makkah, left the town to go to Muḥammad (s.a.w.) and embrace Islām. He did not have to go too far, as the Prophet (s.a.w.) had already come close to Makkah. Indeed, he was delighted to see 'Abbās in the fold of Islām.

Finally, the Muslim army reached al-Zaḥrān, a suburb four miles from Makkah, and decided to camp there. Every one of them was enthusiastically waiting to enter Makkah and visit the House of Allāh. Their camps could easily be seen by the people of the city.

Customarily, many soldiers used to light one fire jointly for cooking purposes. "Tonight, every soldier will light a separate fire," the Prophet (s.a.w.) announced. Observing diligently, the Makkans were bewildered and horrified to notice ten thousand lights at the border of their town. What did it mean? It meant that there were at least fifty thousand Muslim soldiers waiting for the morning to take Makkah. They abandoned the idea of resistance and decided to remain inside their houses when the Muslims entered the city.

An aerial view of Makkah.

"Who is this?" The Muslims spotted a shadow entering their camp. Soon, he was recognized as Abū Sufyān, the archenemy of Islām, who had come to ask the Prophet (s.a.w.) for pardon. "We must not spare Abū Sufyān who has been our bitterest enemy." Some of the *Ṣaḥābah* were enraged to see him. But the Prophet (s.a.w.) forgave him gracefully. Not only that, but he also told Abū Sufyān that anybody who would take refuge in his house, would be safe.

Abū Sufyān could not believe his ears. Was it a dream or reality? How was it possible that the person whom he had persecuted terribly and fought vigorously for many years, would be so generous and forgiving. Within a few seconds, he felt a change in himself. Nothing was left to say except the confession that there is no God but Allāh and Muḥammad is His messenger. He was convinced about the truth of Islām.

The Makkans knew that they had already been defeated. They did not try to resist and shut themselves in their houses. Only 'Ikrimah, with some associates, tried to fight Khālid ibn Waleed, who was his friend before his acceptance of Islām. His attack was answered and soon his party was overpowered by the Muslims.

While entering the city, the Muslims did not boast about this victory. They were reciting, *Allāhu Akbar, Allāhu Akbar* (Allāh is Great, Allāh is Great). The spokesman of the Prophet (s.a.w.) was announcing: "Anyone who takes refuge in the courtyard of Ka'bah or closes the doors of his house, or shelters himself in Abū Sufyān's house, is safe."

It was the second fortnight of the month of Ramaḍān, in the eighth year of *Hijrah*, when the Messenger of Allāh (s.a.w.) entered Ka'bah and demolished all of the false gods placed in it. Indeed, the truth overwhelmed falsehood. Standing at the door-way of Ka'bah, he delivered a speech and recited the following Āyah of al-Qur'ān:

يَـٰٓأَيُّهَا ٱلنَّاسُ إِنَّا خَلَقْنَـٰكُم مِّن ذَكَرٍ وَأُنثَىٰ وَجَعَلْنَـٰكُمْ شُعُوبًا
وَقَبَآئِلَ لِتَعَارَفُوٓا۟ ۚ إِنَّ أَكْرَمَكُمْ عِندَ ٱللَّهِ أَتْقَىٰكُمْ ۚ إِنَّ ٱللَّهَ
عَلِيمٌ خَبِيرٌ ﴿١٣﴾

O mankind, We have created you male and female, and have made you nations and tribes that you may know one another. Indeed, the noblest of you, in the sight of Allāh, is the best in conduct. And Allāh has full knowledge and is well-acquainted (with all things).

al-Ḥujurāt
49: 13

Then he asked:

O people of Quraysh! What do you think of the treatment that I will give you?

The Quraysh replied:

You are a noble brother and son of a noble brother. We expect everything good from you.

The Prophet (s.a.w.) said:

Today, I forgive all of you. You are free to go.

This was unbelievable for the Makkans. They had been pardoned after twenty-one years of animosity with the Muslims. They had been forgiven for torturing and persecuting the *Muhājirūn* and driving them out of their homes.

This was the most peaceful conquest in the history of the world. The whole of Makkah had nothing but appreciation for the Prophet (s.a.w.) and his religion which he had preached against all odds and which was to succeed finally. The Makkans did not have to think any longer. All of them accepted Islām.

The Prophet (s.a.w.) asked Bilāl ibn Ribāḥ to call *Adhān*. From the roof of Ka'bah, the inspiring sound of *Adhān* moved every Muslims' heart. Then he led the *Ṣalāt* in congregation. The conquest of Makkah was the greatest and the most significant victory of the Muslims. It opened avenues for the true faith throughout Arabia.

EXERCISE 18

A. Read each of the following statements carefully and circle the correct answer: a, b, c, or d.

1. The Makkans wanted to fight the Muslims because----
   a. they thought that the Muslims had become weak.
   b. the Muslims had violated the peace treaty.
   c. the Muslims had killed the friends of the Quraysh.
   d. the period of the truce had been over.

2. When the Prophet (s.a.w.) entered Makkah, he -----
   a. imprisoned all of the *Kuffār* living there.
   b. punished those who had persecuted the Muslims.
   c. forced all of the Makkans to accept Islām.
   d. forgave all of the Makkans.

3. The Makkans did not resist the Muslim army in Makkah because-----
   a. they were afraid of the power of the Muslims.
   b. they thought it was useless to fight.
   c. they had no army of their own.
   d. a and b.

B. Answer the following questions.

1. Why did the Makkans violate the peace treaty?
2. Why did the Prophet (s.a.w.) try to deal with the Makkans peacefully?
3. Why did all of the Makkans embrace Islām?

LESSON 19

THE LAST EXPEDITIONS

With the Islamization of Makkah, Ka'bah was cleared of its more than four hundred idols. Five times a day, *Adhān* had taken the place of idol-worshipping. Groups after groups were coming to Prophet Muḥammad (s.a.w.) to declare their faith in *Tawḥeed,* the Oneness of Allāh. The Muslims thanked Almighty Allāh day and night for His help and support against the enemies.

But not everyone was happy. The arrogant tribes of Ḥawāzin and Thaqīf felt the destruction of their idols in Ka'bah as a blow to their pride. They decided to launch a joint attack on the Muslims to bring an end to their power in Makkah. After heavy preparations, their army of 3,000 advanced towards Makkah.

Camping at the entrance of the valley of Ḥunayn, ten miles from Makkah, they made a clever plan to attack the Muslims by surprise. In Makkah, the Muslims heard about this. At once, 12,000 soldiers offered their services to Islām. Among them were two thousand Makkans, who had just embraced Islām. Abū Sufyān was one of them. The same people who had been fighting Islām for many years were now ready to give their lives in supporting and defending it.

Some of the Muslims thought that their huge army would defeat the enemy easily. "This time, we are in great numbers. We will surely be victorious," they said. They did not realize that they needed Allāh's support more than anything else, and numerical strength did not mean absolute victory. It was only their righteousness and absolute trust in Allāh that could make them victorious.

Just before dawn, when the Muslim army was passing through the valley of Ḥunayn and was not yet ready for combat, the two tribes attacked it in the darkness.

The Muslims knew that the Ḥawāzin and Thaqīf were excellent soldiers. This attack caused chaos in their ranks and they ran in different directions. An enemy soldier shouted,"Today is our day of revenge against Muḥammad."

For a few minutes, the Prophet (s.a.w.) stood almost all alone, but he was firm and determined. Then, a number of *Anṣār* and *Muhājirūn* surrounded him, to protect him from enemy spears and arrows.

'Abbās, the Prophet's uncle, called loudly, "O *Anṣār*, who opened their city for Muḥammad; O *Muhājirūn*, who took oath to be sincere to Muḥammad; Muḥammad, the Prophet of Allāh, is still alive. Come forward with him and repulse the enemy."

As soon as the Muslims heard his voice, they forgot about the fear of the enemy and remembered their loyalty to the Prophet. They rearranged themselves and fought until they routed the Ḥawāzin and Thaqīf. They had won another battle but at a very high price this time. Al-Qur'ān makes reference to this event in the following words:

لَقَدْ نَصَرَكُمُ ٱللَّهُ فِى مَوَاطِنَ
كَثِيرَةٍ وَيَوْمَ حُنَيْنٍ إِذْ أَعْجَبَتْكُمْ كَثْرَتُكُمْ فَلَمْ تُغْنِ عَنكُمْ
شَيْـًٔا وَضَاقَتْ عَلَيْكُمُ ٱلْأَرْضُ بِمَا رَحُبَتْ ثُمَّ وَلَّيْتُم
مُّدْبِرِينَ ﴿٢٥﴾ ثُمَّ أَنزَلَ ٱللَّهُ سَكِينَتَهُۥ عَلَىٰ رَسُولِهِۦ وَعَلَى
ٱلْمُؤْمِنِينَ وَأَنزَلَ جُنُودًا لَّمْ تَرَوْهَا وَعَذَّبَ ٱلَّذِينَ كَفَرُوا۟
وَذَٰلِكَ جَزَآءُ ٱلْكَٰفِرِينَ ﴿٢٦﴾

> Surely, Allāh has given you victory in many battlefields and on the day of Ḥunayn, when your great numbers elated you but gave you nothing. The tide overwhelmed you and you ran away in face of the enemy. But Allāh sent His peace upon the Prophet and the Believers. He sent soldiers whom you could not see, and punished those who disbelieved. Such is the reward of the disbelievers.
>
> at-Tawbah
> 9: 25-26

This encounter is known as *Ghazwat-ul-Ḥunayn* (the Battle of Ḥunayn). After this, the Prophet (s.a.w.) returned to Madīnah. Before his departure, he appointed 'Attab ibn Asad, who had accepted Islām immediately after the Prophet's speech, as governor of Makkah.

The Thaqīf tribe took refuge in the town of Ṭā'if in its strong fortress. The Muslims besieged it but lifted the siege after thirty days, and returned to Madīnah.

The victory of Ḥunayn gave more strength to the Prophet (s.a.w.). Many other tribes entered into the fold of Islām. Zayd al-Khayl of the famous tribe of Ṭay' came to Madīnah with a delegation to become a member of the Muslim *Ummah.* The Prophet was delighted to see him. He changed his name from Zayd al-Khayl (increase of horses) to Zayd al-Khayr (increase of goodness).

Hardly had the Muslims enjoyed some peaceful time when the Romans thought of threatening them. They had not forgotten the courageous and steadfast Muslims in the field of Mu'ṭah. Knowledge of the Islamization of Makkah and the rise of Islām in the whole of Arabia, made them anxious. What if the Muslims became too powerful? What if they again dared to attack the Romans? The divided Arabia, with inter-tribal feuds, was a weak neighbor for them, but Arabia united under the banner of Islām was a challenge.

In the ninth year of *Hijrah,* they sent a huge army to invade Arabia and destroy the newly founded Muslim nation. This news brought anxiety for many Muslims. The whole community was mobilized tomake preparations to face the challenge. They gave donations generously. When 'Umar ibn al-Khaṭṭāb brought half of his assets for the war fund, the *Ṣaḥābah* appreciated his generosity, but what about Abū Bakr Ṣiddīque, who brought all of his assets the next day? When someone asked him, "O Abū Bakr! have you left anything for yourself?" he answered, "For me, only Allāh and His Messenger are enough." Such was the spirit of those Muslims and this was the level of their selflessness, which took the banner of Islām to every corner of the world.

The Prophet (s.a.w.) wanted to face the enemy on the border of Arabia rather than inside it, although the time was unfavorable for a long journey. It was the hottest period of the year and a famine had added to the difficulties of traveling. But the *Ṣaḥābah* were not afraid of the hardships in the way of Allāh. Some of the *Munāfiqūn* showed their reluctance to undertake such a tedious journey. At that time, the *Waḥī* came:

فَرِحَ ٱلْمُخَلَّفُونَ بِمَقْعَدِهِمْ خِلَٰفَ رَسُولِ ٱللَّهِ وَكَرِهُوٓاْ
أَن يُجَٰهِدُواْ بِأَمْوَٰلِهِمْ وَأَنفُسِهِمْ فِى سَبِيلِ ٱللَّهِ وَقَالُواْ لَا

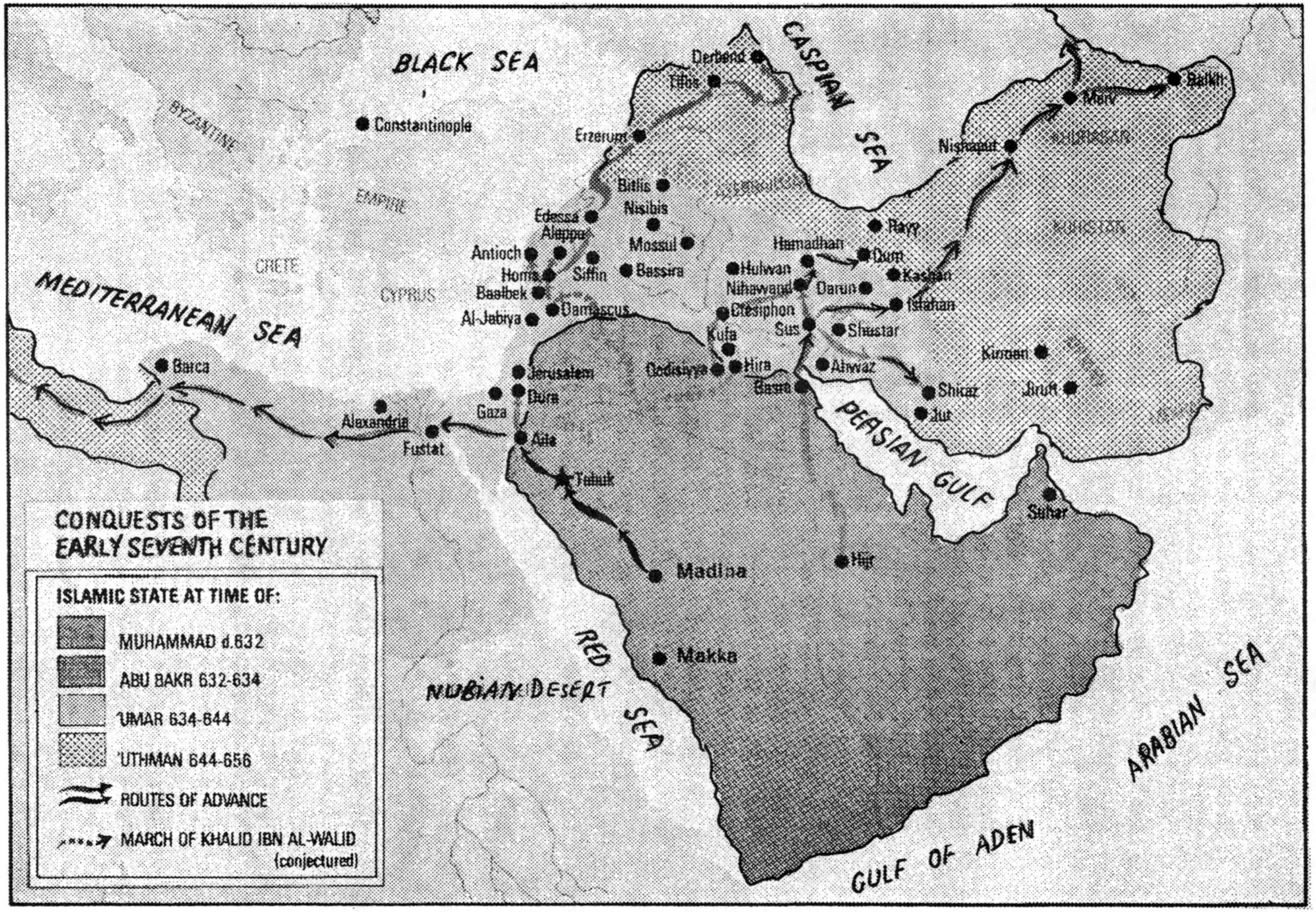

Map of Arabia showing Tabūk.

تَنفِرُوا۟ فِى ٱلْحَرِّ ۗ قُلْ نَارُ جَهَنَّمَ أَشَدُّ حَرًّا ۚ لَّوْ كَانُوا۟
يَفْقَهُونَ ﴿٨١﴾ فَلْيَضْحَكُوا۟ قَلِيلًا وَلْيَبْكُوا۟ كَثِيرًا جَزَآءًۢ
بِمَا كَانُوا۟ يَكْسِبُونَ ﴿٨٢﴾

Those who were left behind in (the Tabūk expedition) rejoiced their inaction behind the Messenger of Allāh. They hated to strive and fight, with their goods and their persons,in the Cause of Allāh. They said, 'Do not go forward in the heat.' Say, 'The fire of Hell is fiercer in heat.' If only they could understand. Let them laugh a little; they will cry much, as the reward of what they used to do.

at-Tawbah
9: 81-82

It was only on such critical moments that the *Munāfiqūn* could be recognized. They tried to convince others to give up the plan of expedition to the north, but in vain. The Muslims' strong faith in Allāh was not to be influenced by worldly considerations.

Passing through the valley of Qurā, and desert of al-Hijr, the Muslim army reached its destination, Tabūk. The combined Syrian and Roman forces were shocked to see the soldiers of Islām. It was beyond their imagination that the Muslims would travel in the harshest conditions to the border of Arabia to repulse their enemy.

"A people, who can endure this journey for the sake of their faith, are impossible to be defeated," they thought. Not long ago, they had tested the courage of the Muslims in the field of Mu'ṭah. Though many times more than the Muslims, the enemy forces could not dare to clash with them. One by one, their commanders began withdrawing without a combat. Almighty Allāh had rewarded His believers for their perseverance and faith. They had won the war without a fight.

The Prophet (s.a.w.) stayed in Tabūk for about twenty-four days. Delegations from various tribes kept on coming to him to embrace the true religion. This expedition contributed a lot towards the expansion of Islām in Syria and her neighbors.

By this time, Islam had spread throughout the Arabian Peninsula. There was a continuous stream of people pouring in Madīnah to accept Islām. Tribe after tribe came to the Prophet (s.a.w.) to declare allegiance to the religion of *Tawḥeed.*

EXERCISE 19

A. Read each of the following statements carefully and circle T if the statement is true or F if it is false.

1. The *Anṣār* were happy to see their old houses in Makkah. T/F
2. All idols placed in Ka'bah were broken by the Muslims. T/F
3. The Thaqīf came to Makkah to embrace Islām. T/F
4. The two enemy tribes attacked the Muslims jointly. T/F
5. 'Abbās reminded the Muslims of their loyalty to the Prophet (s.a.w.). T/F
6. The Ḥawāzin took shelter in the strong fortress of Ṭā'if. T/F
7. The Romans did not like the spread of Islām in Arabia. T/F
8. The Prophet (s.a.w.) did not go to Tabūk with the Muslim army. T/F
9. The Romans assembled to fight the Muslims. T/F
10. The Romans and the Muslims fought at Tabūk. T/F

B. Answer the following questions.

1. Why did the Thaqīf and Ḥawāzin tribes attack the Muslims?
2. What did the *Waḥī* tell the Muslims about the Battle of Ḥunayn?
3. Why did the Roman army not dare to fight the Muslims?

LESSON 20

THE FAREWELL PILGRIMAGE
(*ḤAJJAT—UL—WADĀ'*)
10 A.H.

It was the tenth year of *Hijrah* when Prophet Muḥammad (s.a.w.) made up his mind to lead the Pilgrimage (*Ḥajj*) delegation to Makkah. Hearing about the Prophet's intentions, the whole of Arabia began enthusiastic preparations for the sacred obligation. How fortunate were these Muslims and how precious was this opportunity! Nobody wanted to miss this, not knowing that it was the Last Pilgrimage by the Messenger of Allāh and the time for him to meet his Creator was very near.

More than one hundred thousand people followed the Prophet (s.a.w.) to the sacred city, Makkah. It was a congregation much bigger than Arabia had ever seen. Everyone was absorbed in the remembrance of Allāh and passionate prayers. It was the Prophet's first performance of a full pilgrimage. "Follow me in the performance of your *Ḥajj,*" he told his followers. Each one of them tried his best to be close to the Prophet (s.a.w.) and be in his company. Their love and devotion for him seemed to be increasing every second.

After the performance of *Ḥajj,* the Prophet (s.a.w.) rode his camel, al-Qaswah, to the mount of 'Arafāt. From there, he delivered a *Khuṭbah* which touched the heart of every Muslim. Rabiāh ibn Umayyah repeated his speech sentence by sentence so that everyone could hear it. The Prophet (s.a.w.) said:

> All praises are due to Allāh. We praise Him and desire His help and forgiveness, and we turn to Him and make regrets to Him. We seek His protection against the evils of our souls and the evils of our acts.
>
> O People! listen to my words, for I may not be with you next year. Your lives, your property, and your honor are sacred to you until the Day you meet your Creator. Indeed, you will be held responsible for your actions.

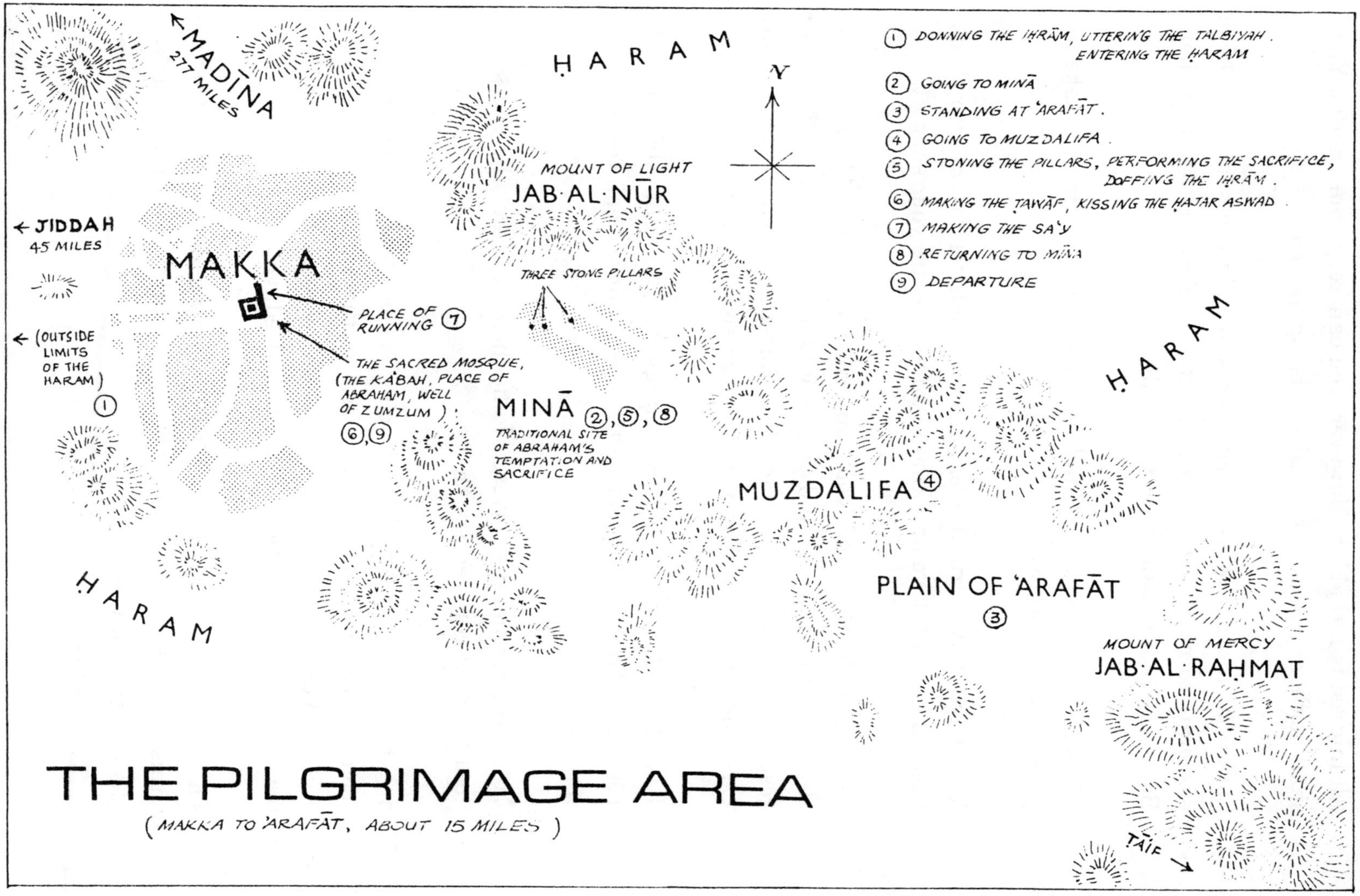

Map of Makkah showing Pilgrimage area.

Whoever is keeping a trust of someone else shall return it to his rightful owner.

All interest is forbidden. However, you can keep your capital. You shall neither oppress, nor shall you be oppressed.

Satan has lost all hopes of being worshipped in this land, but he is desperate to misguide you regarding your deeds other than that. Beware of him to safeguard your religion.

All believers are brothers, and it is unlawful for a man to take the property of his brother without his consent.

Your wives have a right over you and you have a right over them. Treat them with love and kindness for they are your support.

Your Lord is One and your ancestor was one. All of you are descendants of Adam, and Adam was made of clay. The most respectable of you is the one who is most pious. No Arab has any excellence over a non-Arab, and vice-versa, except in piety.

I am leaving among you two things: the Book of Allāh and the conduct of His Prophet (*Sunnah*). If you follow them, you will never go astray.

Help the poor and the slaves. Clothe them as you clothe yourselves; feed them as you feed yourselves.

During his moving speech, the Prophet (s.a.w.) repeated many times: "Have I communicated, O Allāh! be witness." At the end, he said, "O Allāh! I have conveyed Your Message and completed my work." The assembly of the people announced with one voice, "Yes, indeed, you have."

This *Khuṭbah* of the Prophet (s.a.w.) is the greatest declaration of human rights on this earth. It is the best code of life in the world, for the individuals as well for the society as a whole.

Soon after this *Khuṭbah,* Allāh revealed the last and the final Āyah of al-Qur'ān:

ٱلْيَوْمَ أَكْمَلْتُ لَكُمْ دِينَكُمْ وَأَتْمَمْتُ عَلَيْكُمْ نِعْمَتِي وَرَضِيتُ لَكُمُ
ٱلْإِسْلَٰمَ دِينًا

This day, I have perfected your religion for you and completed My Favor unto you, and have chosen Islām as your religion.

al-Mā'idah
5: 3

On hearing these words, Abū Bakr had the feeling that with the completion of the mission, the beloved Prophet (s.a.w.) would soon depart this world. He became sad with the very idea of separation from him.

EXERCISE 20

A. Read each of the following statements carefully and circle T if the statement is true or F if it is false.

1. The Prophet (s.a.w.) performed his Last Pilgrimage in 7 A.H.
2. The Prophet asked the Muslims to follow him in the Pilgrimage.
3. Over one hundred thousand Muslims performed this Pilgrimage.
4. The Arabs were used to seeing congregations of this size.
5. The Prophet's camel was called al-Qaswah.
6. The Last *Khuṭbah* was the best declaration of human rights.
7. The *Khuṭbah* of the Prophet (s.a.w.) had deep effect upon the Muslims.
8. No Muslim liked to be separated from the Prophet (s.a.w.).
9. The Prophet (s.a.w.) delivered his Last *Khuṭbah* inside Ka'bah.
10. The last Āyah of al-Qur'ān was revealed in 8 A.H.

B. Answer the following questions.

1. Where did Prophet Muḥammad (s.a.w.) deliver his Last *Khuṭbah?*
2. What was the last *Waḥī* revealed to the Prophet (s.a.w.)?
3. Write an essay on the Last *Khuṭbah* of the Prophet (s.a.w.).

LESSON 21

COMPLETION OF THE MISSION

After *Ḥajj*, the Prophet (s.a.w.) returned to Madīnah. He had to manage the affairs of a large *Ummah* of the Muslims, which had begun expanding beyond Arabia. He sent many teachers with great knowledge of al-Qur'ān to distant territories.

His health was deteriorating rapidly. Twenty-three years of ceaseless work was taking its toll. The poison which had been given to him in food by an enemy a few years ago, was showing its effects now.

The *Ṣaḥābah* were anxious to see his state. He was everything for them: their father, their guide, their educator, and their Prophet. He was the one who had brought a complete transformation in their lives, from a life of ignorance and barbarism to a life of knowledge and humaneness. He had shown them the right way, the way to be happy in this world and in the *Ākhirah*. His departure was unimaginable for them.

The Prophet's illness became serious and his strength began failing. One day, he found it difficult to walk to the Mosque. With the support of 'Alī and 'Abbās, he walked slowly to the Mosque. This was the last prayer that he led three days before his departure from this world. In his address, he told his followers:

> O Muslims! if I have caused trouble to anyone of you, here I am, to answer for it. If I owe anything to anyone, all I may happen to possess belongs to you.

At that moment, he again directed the Muslims to be always careful about their duties to Allāh. Then he recited the following Āyah of al-Qur'ān:

تِلْكَ الدَّارُ الْآخِرَةُ نَجْعَلُهَا لِلَّذِينَ لَا يُرِيدُونَ عُلُوًّا فِي الْأَرْضِ

وَلَا فَسَادًا ۚ وَالْعَاقِبَةُ لِلْمُتَّقِينَ ﴿٨٣﴾

That Home of the Hereafter, We shall give to those who intend not high-handedness or mischief on this earth. And the End is best for the righteous.

al-Qaṣaṣ
28: 83

When his fever did not let him rise from bed, he asked Abū Bakr to lead the prayers in the Mosque. His illness increased and finally, saying: "O Allāh! The Blessed Companion on High," the Last and Final Messenger of Allāh returned to his Creator. He was sixty-three years old at that time. May Allāh bestow immeasurable peace and blessings on him.

The *Ṣaḥābah* in Madīnah were in such a state of shock that some of them refused to believe that the Prophet (s.a.w.) was dead. "How could the Prophet die?" 'Umar, out of his deep love for the Prophet (s.a.w.), said: "The Prophet is not dead. The news of his death is a false rumor." Then Abū Bakr came in and made a brief speech. After praising Allāh, he said: "If you worship Muḥammad (s.a.w), know that he is dead. But if you worship Allāh, then know that Allāh is alive and He will never die." Then Abū Bakr recited the following Āyah of the Glorious Qur'ān:

وَمَا مُحَمَّدٌ إِلَّا رَسُولٌ قَدْ خَلَتْ
مِن قَبْلِهِ ٱلرُّسُلُ ۚ أَفَإِي۟ن مَّاتَ أَوْ قُتِلَ ٱنقَلَبْتُمْ عَلَىٰٓ أَعْقَٰبِكُمْ ۚ
وَمَن يَنقَلِبْ عَلَىٰ عَقِبَيْهِ فَلَن يَضُرَّ ٱللَّهَ شَيْـًٔا ۗ وَسَيَجْزِى ٱللَّهُ
ٱلشَّٰكِرِينَ ﴿١٤٤﴾

Muḥammad is no more than a Messenger; many messengers passed away before him. If he dies or is slain, will you turn back on your heels? He who turns back on his heels, does not the least harm to Allāh. And Allāh will reward the thankful.

Āl-e-'Imrān
3: 144

Abū Bakr's speech had a deep impact on the people. It removed all uncertainty that they had about the death of the Prophet (s.a.w.), and helped them in recovering from the shock. They regained their senses and reflected over what Abū Bakr had just told them.

The Prophet (s.a.w.) was buried in his wife, Ā'isha's *Ḥujrah,* in the *Masjid-un-Nabawī,* the place where he had breathed his last breath. His mission was completed but his followers' mission had just started: to spread the eternal Message to all corners of the world.

EXERCISE 21

A. Read each of the following statements carefully and circle the correct answer: a, b, c, or d.

1. Islām spread rapidly due to-----
   a. the excellent personality of Prophet Muḥammad (s.a.w.).
   b. the knowledgable teachers which the Prophet (s.a.w.) sent to different places.
   c. the devotion and sincerity of early Muslims.
   d. All of the above.

2. At the time of his death, the Prophet (s.a.w.) was-----
   a. fifty-three years old.
   b. sixty-three years old.
   c. seventy-three years old.
   d. eighty-three years old.

B. Answer the following questions.

1. What did the Prophet (s.a.w.) tell his followers after his last prayer in the Mosque?
2. Why did 'Umar refuse to believe the news of the Prophet's death?
3. How did Abū Bakr pacify the Muslims who were in a state of shock?
4. What is every Muslim's duty in this world?